Dedi

Many o

But sc

We'll just keep it between ourselves, shall we?

Acknowledgements

This compilation has been in the planning stages for at least a decade, and it would never have been completed without the help of a lot of generous friends. Much of the final push has been supplied by friends and fellow parishioners at the Congregational Church of Littleton, who enrich my life every day. Holly Bell, Wayne LaSante, and Rondi Sapporetti and especially Mary Ann and Bob Hanna, went far above and beyond the scope of the World Service Committee to work on this project; proceeds from the sales will be shared with the Church. My writing alter ego, Nancy "Flora" Cooper, took the author pictures and designed the cover, evaluated and typed many of the columns, and held my hand (sometimes virtually or by cell phone) through the doubting moments. Other columns were typed by Patty Schremmer, Bobbie Myles, Rondi Sapporetti, and Mary Ann Hanna. Bob and Merlene Smith, Tyler Golisano, and Liberty posed for the cover picture. There was a long list of folks who evaluated columns and rated them thumbs up or down. Many are Church friends and others are colleagues at the Lincoln Public Library, where I've worked for the past dozen years. I don't dare try to list individuals because I know I would forget someone and feel bad about it for years. I don't need that kind of guilt, so know how grateful I am to all of you. I would be remiss if I didn't also thank my daughters, who provided much of the grist for this column mill, and my Mom, who has always believed in me. And the last shall be first: my husband Ray, the foundation of it all, in whose honor I have based the sections on the vows we exchanged on May 16, 1970. Who knew where it would lead?

How It All Started

Sometime in 1980 my first column was published in the *Littleton (Massachusetts) Independent*. That week two people asked me if I was planning to publish a compilation. Talk about optimistic! Of course, one of them was my Mother, so maybe we can chalk it up to faith. The other woman of faith was Reita Bean, then-librarian of the Reuben Hoar Library, a beloved sanctuary from motherhood, needy dogs, and cranky motor vehicles. Or cranky dogs and needy motor vehicles. But always motherhood.

Many things have changed in the intervening decades. Some things, though, have not changed: same husband, same house, and Mom. For almost 23 of those years, the Brackens lived our lives on the editorial pages of the Littleton newspaper and often its sister publications. People felt like they knew us—and they did. What you read was what there was.

Regularly, folks asked me where on earth I got my ideas, week after week, for all those columns. I always replied, "Living!" To be more specific, one husband, two daughters, 12 cats, three dogs, a dozen vehicles, two hamsters, a bunch of goldfish, several rabbits, and a house. Friends, neighbors and countrymen. A multitude of libraries. Church stuff. League of Women Voters. Vacations, some more relaxing than others. All grist for the column mill.

I have often quipped that writing a column is cheaper than therapy, safer than demon rum and illicit pharmaceuticals, and just as liberating.

Many times I would be struggling with some minor disaster, mumbling to myself through clenched teeth, "Some day we'll laugh about this."

That day usually came—and has come again. Here are some favorite columns, mostly funny but a few sad or introspective ones I threw in to see if you're paying attention. I hope you will laugh today, too.

Jeanne Munn Bracken, 2005

Dearly Beloved

Just Mollie and Me

The summer is well underway. The shakedown cruise, in fact, was last Sunday's roller-skating party. Mollie "won" from the rink the privilege of taking eight of her best friends (in case her parents are too smart to don shoes with wheels...) for an evening of fun. Skate rental and food not included. We settled for two friends. I piled the three girls into the car and collected a gazillion "Mother Points."

We arrived at the rink at 6:02 p.m. I spent the next 10 minutes on my knees, lacing three pairs of skates. At 6:13 I was asked for the first time when we would get pizza. I spent from 6:14 to 6:56 p.m. unjamming various "games" and arguing with one kid about slush puppies versus soda with pizza. There was some cotton candy pressure in there, too, but you get the picture.

At about 7 I order the pizza and soda, promising them slush puppies just before we left. Two of the kids skated for maybe 10 minutes, but Mollie never rolled a wheel at all. She just scooted from game machine to snack bar to game machine. In all, the free party cost about $21, not counting gas, and I figured it was a pretty good deal. Just before we left I got them slush puppies, which they promised not to spill in the car, and then they redeemed their game tickets for guitars, which turned out to be whistles. I made dire threats to pull over and surgically implant the whistle into anyone who dared to blow it in the car. Before we were out of the parking lot, Mollie spilled her slush puppy in the car. A fine time was had by all.

The same can be said for our outing to Maine a couple of days later. We packed up the car, just Mollie and me, and headed for a favorite beach for an overnight camping trip. I figured an air mattress in a tent for one night – how bad could it be? Just to be safe, I borrowed a second air mattress, a double one, from a friend. We loaded the car with cooler, firewood, chairs, and the rest, and set off.

About halfway up the interstate, all of a sudden a helicopter hovered over the car. Except the "helicopter" sound was a flat tire. I found the well-illustrated manual that told how to change the tire. I probably would have been all right, except that the tire had last been changed by King Kong and I hadn't a prayer of loosening the lug nuts. A Good Samaritan came along, changed the tire, and refused any recompense.

We found a tire store within a couple of miles and in just over an hour were back on our way. I had by then unloaded and reloaded the cooler, the firewood, and the chairs twice more. Nobody ever has a flat with an empty car, right?

So we got to the campground only 1½ hours later than planned. Plenty of time to set up, take a swim, get dinner, maybe walk to the beach, then have our campfire-...Uh oh, major snag. We spent the next 90 (count 'em!) minutes pumping up the double air mattress. Finally we just decided it was good enough, skipped the beach walk, got dinner followed by a swim (well, to be honest, I stuck to the hot tub...), went back to the campsite and started the fire.

Major snag II, we've been to this place twice before, in spring and fall. We have never been there before in summer. We expected more people this time of year, but we never thought about flying wildlife. We had not packed bug spray, the screen house, citronella candles or (our newest concession to "roughing it") our bug zapper. We had company. LOTS of company, flying variety, although the fire helped some.

Mollie reminded me about the time on vacation she had an earache and I sang to her all night long. She wanted me to sing to her again. But she didn't like my repertoire. She didn't want to hear "The Water is Wide" or "Michael Row the Boat Ashore" or "Shenandoah." She stood for one chorus of "Kum Bah Yah," then insisted on hearing "My Country Tis of Thee" several times through.

She started asking about 10 when we were going to bed, but the fire was going pretty well by then and I didn't want to waste it. The security guy in the golf cart (talk about déjà vu!) came about 10:45, though, and said it had to be doused by 11, so I gave up fighting the world and hit the sack. Mollie got the single air mattress and I took the double. I discovered at the bottom of her sleeping bag the wet tee shirt she'd worn in the pool and I chastised her for dumping it there. My criticism, however, turned out to be premature, and I managed to slaughter nearly every single mosquito that had accompanied us into the tent with that wet shirt.

By 1 a.m. it had become clear that either we had quit inflating the double air mattress much too soon or it had been infected by the trouble with the tire. I knew I would never sleep on it. Luckily, Mollie was willing to switch and the night passed.

That day we managed to hit both the pool and the nearby beach, where I was unceremoniously reminded about the frigid temperature of Maine ocean water in June. My legs are still numb to about midcalf.

On the way home Mollie asked if we can go again next year. Like a tradition, she said.

I said I was game.

And take two or three friends, she added.

Like the roller-skating party, right?

In a pig's eye.

7

Art Linkletter can't have her

Remember Art Linkletter? The television guy who said, "Kids say the darndest things"? I don't know where he's been lately, but a while ago he had a talk show and among his guests were the cutest little kids you ever saw.

Not only were they cute, but they were really bright. Smart. Clever. Funny. I didn't see the show very often, but I liked that part so much that I bought Linkletter's book of kid interviews—called, what else, *Kids Say the Darndest Things*. I think there was even a sequel, and I read that book, too.

Because Linkletter got kids to say some really wonderful things. They would talk about school, or their brothers and sisters. They would talk about home. Mostly they would talk about their families. They would say the darndest things about their parents.

I thought that was all devastatingly funny. I whooped and hollered when these kids tattled about their parents' sex lives and what Daddy really thinks about the boss. That was, of course, before I had any kids of my own. Knowing what I do now, if my kids were scheduled to appear on Art Linkletter's show, I would petition the Federal Communications Commission to take the show off the air immediately. I don't know what I would use for a reason—probably cruel and unusual punishment or something equally earth-shattering. But I'm sure I'd be able to think up something on the spur of the moment. Panic does that to me.

I don't have enough space to recount all the tales that Mollie has told on me; suffice it to say, some of them have been beauts. Heaven knows I pour out my soul into this newspaper every week, but even I have some deep dark secrets I'd just as soon not see revealed. Or should I

8

say I **had** some secrets, back in the days before Mollie learned to talk?

Really, I love her to pieces, but I'm afraid to take her places because I never know quite what she's going to do. Or say. I'm not even safe in church, because she's been known to make comments that can be heard throughout the congregation. Clearly.

Fortunately, last week's episode didn't happen in church. She and I were checking out a crowded new discount drug store when I reached down to a bottom shelf to buy the latest issue of *Reader's Digest.* Mollie, trotting along behind at a good clip because we were running a tad late, screeched to a halt and grabbed the magazine next to mine on the shelf.

"LOOK, MOMMY," she said in a voice loud enough to be heard in the next county. "NAKED WOMEN. I LOVE NAKED WOMEN. CAN WE BUY IT? HUH? HUH? CAN WE?"

When the floor didn't open up and claim me, I opened my eyes and looked at what she was holding. Strictly speaking, it wasn't a girlie magazine, because the two people on the cover were indeed clad. Sort of. But they were the two most greased-up, muscle-bound people I had ever seen. A man and a woman, each wearing barely (if you will) enough to get the magazine a place on the lowest shelf of a discount drug store display rather than in a plain brown wrapper behind the counter where you have to ask for it.

"No, dear," I said quietly, seizing her firmly by the hand. "Put it back and we'll go now."

"OKAY," she said, "WHERE'S *PENTHOUSE?*"

Obviously the proper response would have been to drop the child's hand and head for the next aisle, making some loud comment when I was far enough away to disown her about the way **some people** raised their children. But I was too busy turning red and stuttering.

9

There are no issues of *Penthouse* in our house. There never have been any issues of *Penthouse* in our house. Nor any of its sister publications. I'd love to know where she learned about *Penthouse*.

If Art Linkletter is reading this, forget it. You can't have her on your show. Instead, I offer you our little friend Josiah, aged about three. One day last week I was sitting by Josiah in a group of like-aged little angels, who were coloring a mural of Spring. Most of the other kids were older and even a poor art critic like me could identify their drawings—tulips, trees, a purple snake.

Josiah sat there for quite a while, drawing an ever-larger circle of purple, yellow and green scribbles. I watched him for a bit.

"That's nice, Josiah," I said. "It reminds me of our back yard in the spring. Purple hyacinths and yellow daffodils bloom right in the green grass. Just like your picture."

Josiah regarded me solemnly for a moment, then burst my bubble. "It's an elephant," he said.

*2005 update: Nearly 20 years later, the tables have turned. Mollie is sometimes reluctant to go any place with me because she can't be sure what **I** will say. Life is sweet.*

Fractious Felines

As promised, and because it seemed like a good idea at the time, the Brackens have acquired another cat. Previously when cats came into our lives, you may recall, they acquired us rather than vice versa.

Snickelfritz appeared, a scared kitten, in the garage on a fall day and Phantomweeniebob wandered in with some trick-or-treaters on Halloween. The latter, as it turns out, is named Schmooz and belongs to neighbors, to whose house we now regularly return him when he sneaks in. He isn't allowed to stay and play with the resident felines because, frankly, he hasn't learned good visitor manners yet. Given his way, he'd eat all the food, then terrorize the others before throwing himself on our laps and turning on his motor.

Phantomweeniebob is hard to resist if you're a human, but I can't say the same if you're a cat whose territory has been invaded. Frankly, he's what we used to call a "brown nose."

So we put out the word that we were in the market for a cat. You'd think that was all it would take, cats being a drug on the market, but apparently not. We had standards. Needs. We wanted an indoor cat and it had to be short-haired because of an allergy flare-up in one of the most important members of the family (me).

We called some of the cat shelters. Finally we thought we'd connected with one humane society, whose ads in a weekly paper showed a couple of appealing felines, pictures and all. The kids wanted "Tiger."

So Ray and Mollie headed off looking for the shelter. They got lost. When they finally found the place, they discovered that there had been a fire and some of the pets had died. Ray was still mad because the place was so hard to find, and Mollie was grief-stricken at the deaths. It was not a fine evening in the Great Cat Search. Back to square one.

A couple of days later a friend gave me a clipping from the same newspaper offering a male neutered cat, grey. An indoor cat. We called the people giving away the cat and got satisfactory answers (short-haired, friendly...) But the owners did not want us to pick up the cat. They wanted to deliver him so they could check out his new home. They arranged to come on Saturday. The Saturday of the Great 1992 Blizzard, as it turned out.

Which is why one night I got a call at work from Lisa, who said they were going to bring him early. The owner also wanted to know what we feed our cat. Lisa didn't have the heart to tell him "whatever's on sale," so named a well-advertised brand that happened to be in the closet at the moment. This cat, the owner said, eats a scientifically-created diet available at feed stores and vets. He'd bring a supply to get us started.

After Lisa reported all that to me, I suggested that it might be well to pick up the house a little.

"I've already started," she replied, leading me to wonder if we shouldn't acquire new pets on a regular basis. As it is, momentous events that set my children to picking up the house unbidden are precious few. No, I decided, the logistics are too terrifying.

Realizing that we were about to adopt a cat we'd never laid eyes on, I said to Lisa, "Gee, I hope we like this cat."

"I'm not worried about the cat," she said, "but I'm not too sure about the owner."

Our fears were unfounded. The owner turned out to be a nice guy concerned about a pet he had to give up. Fair enough. So Drakkar (named, it appears, for an aftershave) arrived, complete with scientifically-formulated food and a handsome scratching post that matches his fur. It also matches the carpet in the dining room, and the significance of that coincidence will become apparent in a minute.

Anyway, we passed muster, Drakkar joined the

12

household, and when I got home from work, I was eager to make his acquaintance.

The feeling was not mutual.

"Where is he?" I asked.

"In the fireplace." So he was, growling and hissing at anyone who approached. Some friendly cat. (The fireplace, you must understand, is empty.)

While trying to get him to come out, we pondered the notion of naming a cat for an aftershave. I've never smelled the stuff, myself, but of my friends who are familiar with it, the vote is even: half love it, half emphatically don't. In choosing such a name, were the owners hoping to improve the aura of the litter box? Beats me. My major impression of the name is that, while classy, it doesn't have much going for it in the "here kitty kitty" sweepstakes. It doesn't exactly trip off the tongue like "Here, Snicky" does. (We never summoned Phantomweeniebob by his full name, since each of us had our own ideas of his moniker and now we know to call him Schmooz. As in, "Schmooz! Come out from under that bed!"

Anyway, Drakkar has a tentative new name. Warf. I'm told the original Warf is a character on Star Trek that growls a lot, so it seems appropriate for the moment.

After a full 24 hours in the fireplace, Drakkar/Warf adjourned to the dining room, where we couldn't spot him after dark and often not before, either. He has now decided he likes my office just fine and I'm trying not to think what cat fur will do to computer disks. He's starting to come around, mostly with the aid of a dangled red Christmas ribbon, and even when he's maddest at us (which at first was all the time) he's never clawed anybody.

I guess this is what happens when you get a used model, instead of a new one.

13

The Canoeing Fool

I went canoeing once, a couple of years ago. Junior high youth group, placid Sudbury River, rained all day. The worst problem arose when the underage Mollie refused to get in the canoe because there was a spider in it. And I still enjoyed it.

So when my brother called to invite us canoeing on the Pemigewasset River in the White Mountains, I was eager, Mollie was willing (as long as there were no spiders in the canoe), while Ray and Lisa reserved judgment. "Pemigewasset" (nobody can pronounce it, nobody can spell it), incidentally, is the Indian word for "white man canoe fool."

By the time the day dawned sunny and warm, Ray remembered that he had hurt his back once when he went canoeing in college, and Lisa looked at the clock, noted it was 7:30 a.m., and rolled over. Mollie (reassured repeatedly that there would be no spiders) and I joined my mother, my brother, his wife, and their two sons (6 and 2), and headed for the river. We left the ponchos and umbrellas in the car on the sunny riverbank, stashed cameras and the like in sealable plastic bags, stuffed sweat-shirts and towels in backpacks, slathered on sunscreen, and shoved off.

But not before my brother gave me an instant lesson on steering a canoe. I was to be the rudder in our canoe – the one with Mollie, Mom and me. I was, after all, the "experienced" canoeist in our craft. Mom, at 72, was trying it for the first time ever. Now you have to understand about my Mom. She may be semi-retired, but she's a trooper; she has climbed mountains that daunt people half her age, she walks and gardens and stacks wood, and she's willing to try about anything. We agreed that we understood perfectly our respective roles in the canoe propulsion business. We just weren't sure we'd actually be able to do it on the spur of the second as need arose.

We're not talking whitewater canoeing here; the Pemi is, to put it mildly, not deep at this time of year, with frequent stretches of ripples at the shallowest points. But it's no Sudbury River. There would be, my brother made it clear, "challenges."

The first "challenge" came about 100 feet after shoving off; we had to steer through some rocks. We could see exactly what we should be doing; the canoe, however, had other plans. We got hung up, got loose, and got underway leaving only a little paint behind for those who follow. It was not the only paint on those rocks. It was not the only paint we left that day.

But we did pretty well, all in all. We never went through any "ripples" backward, we never went sideways, we only broadsided my brother's canoe once, and I only had to leap overboard into the knee-deep water a couple of times. The real problem was the thunderstorm.

We were having lunch on a sandbar in full view of a golf course, joking about the golf balls in the water (some water hazard!) when the first rumbles were heard. No problem. Not even close. We continued on our leisurely way, watching wild duck families nearly walking on water in their frenzy to escape us. Pointed out the similarities between the cliff swallow dwellings in mud banks and the human condos above. Paid (real) bread to a toll duck for the privilege of passing on his river. Bailed the canoes occasionally with the only scoop we had, a Frisbee.

When the storm reached us, we paddled to shore and holed up under overhanging trees, sitting on rocks. We were not alone. Sharing a nearby rock was the biggest spider I've ever seen outside of a terrarium, as big as the palm of my hand. Luckily Mollie didn't see it. After a few minutes the rain abated and we continued. We pulled in for another shower, then reached the only really dangerous stretch on our route. We knew it was dangerous because there were three signs warning of downed trees. I "knew" however, that the trees had been cut and the river was open, so I didn't worry.

Only after we'd accidentally grounded and been rescued by my brother, who took the canoe past the trees for us, did he mention casually that the signs had been put up after the trees were removed, that a family had capsized at that point the day before. By then we were in Fat City, nearing the end of our nine-mile journey.

By then we were also soaked to the skin, because the rain had started again and showed no sign of letting up. I thought longingly of the poncho I'd left in the car with Mr. and Ms. "Thanks But We'd Rather Watch Videos." Sunscreen washing from my forehead into my eyes caused a lot of tears, which didn't matter anyway, because my glasses were so wet and fogged that I took them off and paddled the last mile with my bad eye closed.

We took pictures of the expedition at lunch on the sandbar, carefully framed to show the canoes in the background. We took pictures back at the car, too, before I found a way to dry my glasses but after my six-year-old nephew rolled in the mud. It looks like the before-and-after pictures of "The Poseidon Adventure."

Would I go canoeing again?

Sure.

But I'd advise sticking to rivers you can spell.

1997

Family Ties

This was the first meeting of Ray's family of origin in 53 years.

Those who have been following the saga of Ray's family are no doubt hankering to hear how the great reunion went. It was, in a word, a blast.

But since it was a Bracken family vacation, it was naturally not without its moments of ... excitement. Luckily, the excitement didn't start until we got to our destination. I say "luckily," because I do not like to fly. My antipathy to flight is partly because of the cramped quarters and partly because there is always a crying child aboard and partly because, darn it, I am a backseat driver, and I want to help the captain fly.

When I spoke to our travel agent, he said that fares were low. Low fares work for me. The only thing worse than being crammed into a tiny seat with some bozo's head reclined into my lap is having to pay the equivalent of a year's tuition for the privilege.

Since we were heading for mid-Nebraska, the route proved to be a little tricky. We were first routed from Boston to Denver to Omaha to Grand Island. For those unfamiliar with geography, that involved going West, then East, then West. Which seemed a little silly to me, especially since the sister flying in from Wyoming was routed Salt Lake City, Omaha, Grand Island. In other words, East then West.

Why, I asked those in the know, did the westerners have to fly over Grand Island and then fly back to the west, while the easterners had to fly over Grand Island and then fly back to the East? The answer was something about connections. The agent offered a change of flights in Minneapolis, St. Louis, or Chicago. I rejected Chicago right off the bat and countered with agreeing to fly into Lincoln and rent a car to get to Grand Island, less than 100 miles away.

The travel agent and I played phone tag with

suggestions and counter offers, and finally, when it came down to a choice between an easy change of flights and a low fare, I bowed to the inevitable (read: cheap) and opted for O'Hare.

I'm no frequent flyer, but I have managed to visit most corners of this country via airplane without ever setting foot in O'Hare, the busiest airport in the world. It was a record I didn't want to ruin. But there it was, and Thursday at noon we found ourselves on what felt like the Walk for Hunger, up one concourse, under a runway approach (honest, underground), and along another concourse. The time between flights was just enough that we didn't have to really run, but we also didn't have time to get something to eat.

This latter fact gains importance when one considers that our "breakfast flight" served honey-mustard pretzels and the beverage of our choice. The luncheon flight served non-honey-mustard pretzels and the beverage of our choice, the selection at that time having expanded to alcoholic libations for those so inclined.

On our return trip, we were pleased (not to mention relieved) to discover that we had indeed chosen a meal flight and were served actually tasty lasagna. We were also, incredibly, amused by one flight attendant's announcements. "Ladies and gentlemen, the seatbelt sign has been illuminated, an indication that the captain has found the airport." Go, United!

Lincoln may be Nebraska's capital, but it is also home to a very small, even homey airport. Everybody seemed to know everybody else. We loved it, as well as the fact that it was about two steps from the luggage carousel to the car rental counter. We were, on the other hand, nonplused to discover what's going as a mid-sized rental car these days. Or maybe we're just spoiled by our van.

Any Bracken vacation by law requires either a medical/dental emergency or an automotive one, but we were sure that this trip would be without any such distractions. For one thing, Ray basically didn't have any teeth left to get abscessed, and the rental car had only 6,000 miles on the odometer, so it was surely in excellent running shape.

We drove from Lincoln to Grand Island in the blink of an eye, which really isn't much of an exaggeration. The speed limit is 75 miles an hour, and folks there don't seem to stick to the limit any better than we Easterners do to 65. We had booked a room at the Midtown Holiday Inn, which turned out to be a lot closer to the interstate than to the middle of any town, and frankly the Jacuzzi temperature was too high, but overall we were pleased.

We met Ray's brother and his sister, a cousin and an aunt; and even the brother from Minnesota who had said he couldn't make it drove in with his wife. Before the whole gang got together, though, we went through the minor disaster that led us to an automotive repair facility. Ray's Grand Island brother is wheelchair-bound and has a van converted for handicapped use. When Ray and I got aboard with him to head to the airport, the hydraulic lift and door malfunctioned, so the guys got to take the motor apart. They didn't fix it, of course, and we drove that van the rest of the weekend with the door open--but hey, it was male bonding, and they even let me hand them the tools.

Just so we'd feel at home, vacation-wise, though, we did have to visit the hospital where Ray's brother was having an infected wound re-dressed.

The relatives, incidentally, are warm and welcoming and funny. So the experience was worth waiting 53 years for.

2005 update: That was the only time all four siblings were together. Both brothers have died .We were really blessed to have that weekend.

Dispatches from the cat house

"Give me your tired, your poor, your huddled masses..." When Emma Lazarus wrote the words inscribed on the base of the Statue of Liberty, she was reportedly referring to immigrants, not, contrary to popular opinion, the propensity of the Brackens to take in stray animals.

At my last report, instead of leftover fries, Lisa had come home from McDonalds with a stray calico cat. The skinny little female had a name (Willow) before she got to the house, which I know from sad experience usually means the critter has found a home.

I didn't give up easily, though. I remembered a friend in Jamaica Plain who mentioned, a couple of years ago, that she might be in the market for a cat.

I e-mailed her before the sun set again. No, she hadn't yet acquired a cat. Yes, she was interested. However, she was going on a book tour and wouldn't be able to take the cat until sometime in July. That was in April, so we bit the bullet, took the cat along with all the others to the vet's for a series of shots.

Willow might have been pitiful-looking, but she was sure feisty. For the first couple of weeks, she battled any four-legged creature that invaded her space (read: my bedroom). That included all three of our other cats plus the cat-chasing, barking fool canine who lives here. Life was not very peaceful at the Bracken homestead.

When the girls took the cats to the vet, they were supposed to make an appointment for neutering Mongo, our most recently arrived male cat. I was hoping that Willow's new owner, whoever s/he might be, could be responsible for her spaying.

You can see it coming. I didn't. After Willow had been here a month or so, she started to fill out nicely. And fill out. And fill out.

"I think she's pregnant," Mollie announced. We all assured her that the cat was certainly not pregnant.

Don't you hate it when your kids are right and you're wrong? I called the vet to find out how long the feline period of gestation is.

Eight weeks. Counting backward, I was somewhat relieved to figure out that Willow had arrived here pregnant.

Hah. By the time Willow had been here 10 weeks, she was still waiting and getting bigger all the time. Mongo and Willow, despite their initial animosity, had apparently put their differences behind them for at least a brief period of time, and we were going to have to deal with the consequences.

Friends told us hair-raising tales of cats giving birth in secluded or just plain inaccessible places. The most colorful was the one who had her kittens in an air duct.

We don't have air ducts here, but I took to closing all the closet doors, afraid she'd choose, say, a pile of clean laundry. Mollie put together a basket with a pillow.

The basket didn't appeal to Willow. At the time of her confinement, last Sunday, she chose the most inaccessible place in the entire house: under Lisa's bed.

What's under there, I asked Lisa.

Magazines, socks…she didn't get too specific, but I could just imagine. Lisa's room is legendary for its messes. Suffice it to say, it was sometime Monday before Mollie called us at work to report that, rather than four kittens, there were five. That's how inaccessible Willow's chosen spot is.

During the birthing process, which took most of the day, Mongo napped on top of Lisa's bed. Every now and then, he'd jump down, look under the bed to see what was going on, then climb back up and go to sleep again. It reminded me of Dad resting at home on the living room couch while Mom was at the hospital giving birth to my brother.

Human fathers don't get away with that anymore, although I suppose it's too much to ask that father cats provide ice chips and coach heavy breathing.

Whatever. Luckily, we have homes lined up for three or four of the kittens and I still have hopes of moving Mother Willow on to Jamaica Plain in a few months.

I don't suppose this is the end of it, either. Mongo still hasn't been to the vet for his little operation. A recent newspaper article reports that there are 79 million cats living in American homes.

Make that 79 million and five.

We are gathered here today

Getting Together, Family Style

I knew before I left that you were skeptical about my vacation plans--about getting together with all those aunts, uncles, and cousins for a reunion; about the 12 hour drive to Pennsylvania; about setting up and taking down the camper three times in as many states over 10 days.

Lots of potential there for disaster, you told me. You'll be happy to know that everything turned out fine. Well, there were a few moments. . .

We had planned to leave at 6 p.m. and actually got on the road around 10:30--a real improvement over last year, when we hoped to get on the road mid-morning and finally pulled out at 3 in the afternoon.

This time things went pretty well until we got to Troy, New York, where we picked up our interim route all right and got the second route before Murphy's Law took effect. That's the one that says: If you are using a 1969 road map, they will have changed all the roads around since then. A corollary to that continues: You will only get lost at 1 a.m., when you will not see anyone you dare ask for directions except the two police cars at the intersection where you go through the red light.

We somehow ended up on the entrance road to the New York Thruway, a route we had already rejected based on previous experience: we didn't want to spend 10 hours betting whether the next sign we saw was "Buffalo 250 miles" or "Deer crossing next 12 miles." (The route would be a lot more interesting if the former were a critter and the latter a town.)

We asked the person at the toll plaza how to get on Route 20. He helpfully said, "It runs parallel all the way to Buffalo," which is akin to saying to a dying man in the Sahara that the Mediterranean is right over the mountains.

To make a long story short, we found ourselves heading

for The Big Apple, got off the highway, and followed a route that looked increasingly familiar--mostly because we'd been there an hour before. We circled the Empire Plaza in Albany twice and crossed the Hudson River three times before we got it right. Take it from me, the capital of New York State has little to recommend it at 2 a.m.

I figured getting lost in Albany was an omen, but things went pretty well after that. The family reunion near Erie, Pennsylvania, was a lot of fun--a little confusing, I admit, but fun. I mean, when you have 42 people from 13 states wandering around, you have to expect a little confusion, don't you?

Just getting everybody sorted out was a big step. There were some cousins-in-law, some second cousins and their kids (I never could figure out all that once-removed and twice-removed stuff), and my first cousins had all had some kids I'd never met before. Then there were my mother's cousins, plus a handful of their descendants.

Who all came, you ask? Now get this straight because I'm not going through it again. Grace, Mike, Pat, Pam, Ray, Candy, Steve, Dick, Diane, Brent, Nathan, Nancy, and Norm. So far, so good. Lisa, Lucia, Laura, and Lil. Two Tims. Two Chris's. Three Bills. A Polly and a Mollie. Two Georges, two Junes, plus Joan, Jonathan, Jud, Judd, Joyce, Jeanne, Judy, Jeff (and his twin Ken). Among the no-shows were another Nathan, Jan, Jack, and Jim. It was a good week before mothers were calling their kids with the right names again.

There were several group events: a church-type dinner (the leftovers fed the gang for 3 days), a brunch, another dinner (we are a long line of eaters). Several had scrounged in their attics and brought boxes of old family photos, including the famous one of the two male cousins taken 25 years ago, showing them brushing their teeth and wearing nothing but socks. Naturally there were people in some of the snapshots nobody could remember.

People spent a lot of time pointing to kids in pictures and asking, "Who's THAT?"

The first day was taken up by lengthy, convoluted explanations of who else was coming, how they were arriving, and when. The last day was taken up by lengthy, convoluted explanations of who was going where from here, when, and with whom. There was a lot of switching-- Lil, Joan, and Jonathan flew in from Florida and were met at the Buffalo airport by Diane and Bill, but left by car with June for Maryland. Things like that.

In the middle there was a motel pool party marked by the telling of a joke so long-winded and just plain bad that it already has become family legend. A significant number of the group took a winery tour (free samples are good bait in our family); then some went antiquing, some golfing, and several went swimming together, but ended up at different beaches.

There were the usual quotient of minor disasters-- one kid got overtired and threw up at dinner, another fell and needed five stitches to put his chin back together. All in all, not a bad record.

Naturally everybody had a camera (Kodak loves family reunions) and hundreds of snapshots plus a few formal portraits will be circulated for a while, then added to boxes in attics in 13 states.

They will be dug out in 20 years when we have another family reunion, and I figure by then we'll all be pointing to the twins and their brother (Keith? Kevin?) from Idaho (or was it Virginia?) and asking, "Who's THAT?"

2005 update: In half a dozen reunions since, no sight of the twins.

Head 'em up, move 'em out (or ride 'em, chaperone)

Now, as promised several weeks ago, here is a report of what your kids have been doing all summer on those day camp buses. I figured I'd have enough material for a column, and I was right.

Day Camp Week Two, Field Trip Number One. We are heading to Boston to the Children's Museum. There are over a hundred kids, probably 30 counselors, one father, and me, all loaded on three buses.

I am on the middle bus with the "middle aged" kids—neither the very youngest nor the pre-teens. We've been on the bus about five minutes when the songs begin. I lean forward to the adult in charge of the bus. "At least it's not 'Jingle Bells' or '99 Bottles of Beer on the Wall,' I murmur. Another five minutes and someone begins a rousing chorus of "Jingle Bells." The summer is off and running.

Another 15 minutes and I hear from the back of the bus, "10,000 bottles of beer on the wall..." Nobody picks up the chorus. Thank heaven!

It is a cool day and those who were smart enough to bring sweatshirts or jackets are smug. Everyone else is cold. Kim wears a beach towel off and on all day. I alternately open and shut the bus windows for the kids.

Day Camp Week Three, Field Trip Number Two. We are going to Canobie Lake Park (and any year now the program will spell it right). I ride on the first bus with the youngest kids. There are several parents along, and I sit with the bus driver's wife in the seat directly behind the operator; there is about two inches of knee room. I do not have two-inch knees. It is not comfortable.

I spend a lot of time opening and shutting windows again. This time there's no singing but a lot of shouting,

27

seat-kicking, and rocking. We have had plenty of time at the school, since some miscommunication has occurred between the camp staff and the bus company, resulting in an hour-long wait. That hour has been spent warning kids to "go" before the buses leave because the ride is a long one. We make it to Westford (maybe three miles) before one of the kids announces he has to "go." Desperately. We stop at a "no-sanitary-facilities" rest area. The kid goes behind a tree, while everyone else is distracted by counting 18-wheelers on the highway, in the opposite direction.

At the amusement park a number of other kids eat lots of junk food, then try out some hair-raising rides. They are very sick. The counselors group them on Bus 3 to go home. I am grateful I'm on Bus 2. I am wet from the Log Flume Ride but otherwise unbowed. I am not yet broken.

Day Camp Week Four, Field Trip Number Three. We are going to see the play "The Princess and the Pea" in Milford, New Hampshire. Coming off a heat wave, we're pretty comfortable. I sit with Josh, who is about seven. We have a discussion about why people take short cuts but never long cuts. Josh doesn't know quite what to make of me. There are two parents on this trip—another mother and me. She follows in her own car. Chicken.

Josh and I have a discussion about favorite Chinese restaurants. Here is common ground. Josh has good taste. We get to the theater. The Prince is a major jerk. The Princess is a feminist. I love it. The Prince gets a cream pie in the face. The kids love it. It was, frankly, totally awesome.

On the way home I get, for the first time, a seat to myself. It is, however, a seat over a wheel well, unsuitable for a person with legs, so it doesn't count. I am forced to spend half of the homeward journey arbitrating a dispute between Kim and Mollie over who's hogging the six-pack cooler, which they are ostensibly sharing as a pillow. I am momentarily sorry I haven't filled the cooler with Coors Light.

Day Camp Week Five, Field Trip Number Four. We are on our way to the New England Science Center in Worcester. The two buses leave on time, but without the usual warning to "go", because the plumbing is out at the school. Our first stop, therefore, is at the Shattuck Street School so everybody can "go". This is essential, because even the bus driver has to "go."

We load 'em up again. Less than a mile down the road, even before we get to Route 495, the lead bus (I am on bus 2) executes a perfect three-point turn. Some important papers have been left behind at Shattuck Street, and we are to go on by ourselves while they retrieve them and follow.

Sounds good. We ask the driver if he knows where the place is. He thinks so. We drive south on Interstate 495. Past Route 290. Okay, I figure the driver knows a short cut. Pass the Mass. Pike. Must be **some** short cut. We get to Upton. We turn around. The driver has been given the wrong directions.

No harm done. We get there. We watch the baby monkeys play in their trees, the polar bears back-stroke in their pool. We have a fine time. I chat on the way home with Stephanie. She shows me how to draw a cube (shaky, because the bus bounces) and I help her spell a message for her first grade teacher. We do not go home by way of Upton.

Day Camp Week Six, Field Trip Number Five, the Grand Finale. Water Country! Nearly every week we have been threatened with rain or at least showers. I have carried two rain ponchos and an umbrella everywhere we've been, and it's worked. Not a drop of rain. I don't plan to take them to Water Country. After all, we're going to get wet anyway, aren't we?

I have had a bit of a scare, actually. A message was sent home a few days ago asking that chaperones drive our own cars. I do not want to drive to Portsmouth. The other parents do not want to ride the bus. The decision: I can, they don't have to. We all get our own way. How nice.

The day dawns. Cold and rainy. Oh, well, I remind myself, we're going to get wet anyway, so what's the difference?

But people begin to back out. Starting with Lisa. She is not alone. The trip is cancelled.

Instead, we can either watch a movie in the morning or go bowling (depending on age—the age of our kids, not us), and in the afternoon we'll all go roller-skating.

I pass. I head home to write this column. Now I'm going to brew a cup of tea and read today's newspaper out on the porch. With my feet up.

So I won't get to ride the buses anymore. And I find....I'm...actually ...disappointed.

You know what? Your kids are great. We've had a terrific summer.

I've had the time of my life.

Rest Assured, the Security Patrol Is

We spent the long weekend at one of those big rallies where hundreds of recreational vehicles and thousands of people gather at the Franklin County fairgrounds where there are only two restroom buildings and six showers to accommodate all. Luckily most of the rigs have their own "facilities," as the long line at the dump stations at the end of the weekend would certainly attest.

Anyway, we got there at about dinner time on Friday and were mellow, looking forward to three days of no television, no telephones, put-your-feet-up relaxing. So when the fellow came to us and said, "We need a security patrol for 1 to 2 a.m. and we'd like you to volunteer," we said "Sure!" We'd seen the scooting golf carts. The job didn't seem too strenuous.

So that evening, someone with a very important-looking paper spent 5 minutes explaining whom we were to relieve at 1 a.m. and whom we were to awaken at 2. We were supposed to wake up the fellow with the birdcages on the table outside his rig and the office supplies mogul with the enormous new rig, who said he'd leave his patio lights on. Piece of cake.

All psyched up, we decided to take a little nap before our shift. We'd been out maybe five minutes when a knock came on the door and the guy with the important paper said, "False Alarm! It's tomorrow night."

"Tomorrow night" came. I dozed in my clothes, figuring I'd take a shower after my shift when there would surely be no competition for the three women's showers. I figured there'd be hot water then, too. 1 a.m. Right on schedule, a tap on the door. Up and at 'em.

Ray dressed for the occasion in a Coast Guard uniform with three stripes. He out- ranked my plain navy sweatshirt, so he got to drive the golf cart.

As we walked to our duty station, Ray said he had heard there may be trouble. The local teens, it transpired, were reportedly spoiling for a fight with the campers' teens. Oh, swell – our very own West Side Story. But I'm no Natalie Wood.

We reported to the main gate. Our instructions: alternately patrol through the big fairgrounds in the golf cart and guard the front gate. Do not let anyone in without a sticker.

Um, we wanted to know, if somebody tries to get in without a sticker, how are we supposed to stop them? Good question. They showed us where the phone was, with the police telephone number.

We were issued our security equipment and costume: an orange mesh vest, three flashlights of the type guys use to park large aircraft, a walkie-talkie, and a golf cart.

We were sent out to patrol. Ray's first stop was the coffee station. We patrolled. We didn't see much, except one large group of campers still up and apparently having a party. "Think we should tell them to break it up," I asked Ray importantly.

"Why?" he said. "That's the deaf mute chapter. Who are they gonna bother?"

Good point. We patrolled some more. Ray couldn't find the headlights on the golf cart, so I used two of the flashlights as headlamps. "If anyone wants to land a jet on the racetrack", I told Ray, "we're all set." We finished our patrol with another stop for coffee.

Then we had gate duty. The other half of our patrol told us that someone had reported a lethal weapons (grapefruits) pelting at an RV. The constabulary had been called. A nice young patrolman showed up, suggested we get the kids' names if we caught them, and headed off to check it out.

He was back in a few minutes. Nothing. He drove off. I asked Ray what we were supposed to do if the trouble-seeking teens showed up, since we were unarmed. I suggested getting grapefruit from our fridge, just in case.

Nobody tried to get in, sticker or no, except the other half of our patrol team, who wanted to know why we didn't answer their call on the walkie-talkie. Because we didn't hear them, we replied. All we could hear on the thing was 100 decibel static. We turned the walkie-talkies off.

Ray got another cup of coffee when we headed down to wake up our replacements for the two to three shift. I woke up the first guy with a single tap. Ray went to the second rig, and went tappity tap. Nothing. Tappity tap tap. Nothing. This went on for maybe ten minutes. "I'll wake him up", I said. Pound, pound, instant success.

We went back to the front gate, turned in our vests, flashlights, walkie-talkie, and golf cart. I headed to the showers. No waiting, plenty of hot water. Ray had another cup of coffee.

We found out in the morning why we had so much trouble rousing our replacements. We'd been told to awaken the wrong people. Our true quarry slept through the night.

I always get nervous when Ray gets his hands on neat toys like those nifty flashlights, or walkie-talkies. He invariably thinks he needs one of his own.

I was partially right. Now he thinks it would be nice to have a golf cart.

2005 update. Ray has survived without a golf cart, but we did give him his very own walkie-talkies for Father's Day. We still can't make them work, which is probably okay, since we have not yet mastered the skill of having them in different, useful locations should the need arise.

Murder (almost) at the museum

I had a feeling it wasn't the brightest idea I'd ever had, but I was committed to it by a promise to my kids. My kids had never been to Harvard Square. Hard to believe, but there it was. I'd been telling them for weeks about how eclectic Harvard Square is, how odd some of the people are, and they wanted to see for themselves. Actually, Lisa just heard there were shops and she was ready to go.

But first, we thought we'd take in the new Whodunit exhibit on forensics at the Museum of Science. A fan of mysteries and true crime, I thought I might pick up a few pointers so I could spot the perp earlier in books.

And this was all a fine idea, really it was. Except that things, as usual, were not as simple as they seemed. First Mollie, then Lisa wanted to take a friend along. The car will only fit one friend comfortably, so after a bit of negotiation (some would call it a bribe), Lisa took her friend along. I did have moment's pause wondering if the library pass to the museum admitted "four in a family" or just "four," because it was clear passing her friend off as one of my kids would be tricky, since she happens to be African American. The pass said just "four," no kinship requirements, and we were on our way.

We parked at Alewife in the rain and got to the museum with a minimum of fuss, although with a maximum of precipitation, umbrella jockeying and poking. There have been dozens of newspaper ads touting the Whodunit exhibit and billboard signs outside the museum drawing in the hoards. Unfortunately, once you are inside, there aren't any obvious directional signs, nor do any of the handouts or daily schedules provide a clue (if you will) how to find the Whodunit-the-exhibit. So we started the experience standing in line waiting to be told where to go.

We were not alone.

34

Whodunit would have been a fascinating exhibit, with its do-it-yourself mystery (solve it, not commit it, although by the end of an hour.... . .) I say "would have" because you have to factor in the school vacation week crowd, the President's Birthday holiday from work crowd, and the Ohmigawd-Mahtha-it's-raining-crowd. Add an ambient air temperature in the gallery of approximately 99 degrees plus swarms of children much too young to comprehend the interactive exhibits but determined to try or at least mess it up for everybody else, and you have the makings of a less than optimum museum experience, not to mention a major flu incubation laboratory.

We gave up on the exhibit and headed for the gift shop, Lisa figuring that any opportunity to spend money should not be missed. Their major purchase involved some freeze-dried astronaut snacks ("Yuck!") that caused serious rethinking of any career path requiring space travel.

We took the T back to Harvard Square, which I used to traverse twice a day on my commute. That was 24 years ago, and while some things have changed, Out of Town Newspapers, The Coop and Das Wursthaus are still anchoring the bricks.

The first major decision was where to have lunch. I steered them to the Wursthaus, explaining that it was the only place outside of Berlin that this old German major had ever found a *Weisse mit Schuss*. I explained that this treat is a glass of white beer with a shot of raspberry syrup. They were unimpressed. It's better than it sounds and I deserve it, I whined. I lost.

We lunched at Pizzeria Uno, and I forgave them their lack of international sophistication once the waitress brought me a 16 oz. glass of fresh-brewed iced tea--in February! Truth be told, I'd take good iced tea over beer any day. However, I began to get alarmed when the waitress kept refilling the glass--at least four times. Mollie swore she had at least six glasses of Coke, so I expected to spend the rest of the afternoon looking for restrooms. Fortunately, the kids have inherited my capacity rather than Mr. Bad Bladder's genes, and he was safely off at work, so the impending disaster never struck.

We hit Tower Records, examined a lot of people with green hair, purple hair, pink hair, and the Telly Savalas look. We skipped CVS (two stores in two blocks-- talk about overkill!). We hit the Army-Navy store, where one display of camouflage equipment touted its appeal for the "Tonya Harding Hit Squad" and a genuine East German Army raincoat went for $20. I was tempted, but olive drab is not my color.

We looked at rude greeting cards at The Coop, rude T-shirts everywhere (some on bodies, some on store racks), and a couple of cosmetic stores. This being Harvard Square, of course everything was politically correct. The endangered species soaps were presumably merely fashioned in the shape of various beasts and not of them--pink elephants, lemon turtles, and (unaccountably) balsam blue whales.

By the time we got to Urban Outfitter (which has a display of farmer overalls in the window...) I was sinking. I expected, given newspaper horror stories of city life, to find MACE, ammo and various weaponry, but the stock ran to colored glass and crude yet attractive journals from India.

Lisa's friend was getting a glazed look in her eyes, Mollie was complaining about sore feet, and I was way past glazed, heading for comatose. Fortunately, right about there Lisa ran out of money so we headed home.

As we walked to the car in the parking garage, both kids turned to me simultaneously, having finally remembered they had been put in charge of reminding me to turn off the lights before leaving for the subway. I let them sweat for a minute before assuring them that someone really clever (*moi*, naturally) had remembered to

36

turn the lights off, anyway. It was malicious, I admit it, but I had to get even somehow.

2005 update: The Coop is now a big box book store outlet and Das Wursthaus, alas, is no more. Pizzaria Uno survives.

1999

Pooling All My Resources

I think it was the Great Pool Debate, resounding around Littleton a few months ago, that first made me aware of water temperature. (A recap for those who have luckily forgotten that fiasco: One faction argued that the optimum temperature for a team pool was several degrees lower than that for a fitness/recreational pool, given as a reason to oppose the project.) Oh, sure, I have adjusted the odd hot water heater in my time, and I've judged various bodies of water as swimming places over the years, but I just dubbed them EEEEK! or AAAAAAH! There isn't much middle ground — er, water — between those categories. Either a swimmer (me) is able to enter the water without shivering, or she is not.

When I came, at the mid stage of my life, to embrace Fitness with a capital F, I naturally turned to water, buoyancy being a definite plus for my muscles and joints. I still didn't pay any attention to the temperature of the water, until I noticed a thermometer hanging off one of the ladders. Eighty-six degrees. That is the magic number throughout the year, although I insist that 86 degrees feels quite different in January than it does in July, taking the ambient air in the pool building into account. All in all, I have become quite fond of 86 degrees (although, to be honest, on the days when I go to the pool after a workout in the gym — and a shower — the water isn't as bracing and cooling as I would wish.)

Last summer, visiting a friend who has a backyard pool, we became quite adept at figuring out the water temperature before looking at the thermometer. Her husband tends to favor a lower temperature and the accompanying lower electric bill, while she and I opt for personal comfort every time, and damn the cost. By the end of the season, the pool was holding steady at about 84 degrees, which was close enough on most occasions.

An indoor pool at a resort where we vacationed in late fall was kept around 80 degrees, which was surprisingly challenging to enter and resulted in leg cramps. It's been several years since I swam at Long Lake (I guess I'm less loath to parade in a bathing suit among strangers than among neighbors), but when I accompanied visiting out-of-state friends to the beach in early July, the water felt quite bath-ish — although I did warn them that springs out near the floats were significantly cooler.

This has been a family summer for us. In mid-July we attended a family reunion (my side of the tree) in New Hampshire's White Mountains. The resort was perfect, right down to the unusual semi-circular pool. The brochure noted that the water is heated to 75 degrees. Now 75 degrees doesn't sound all that painful, but the pool was daunting enough that most of the elders (anybody between the ages of 30 and 85) passed up a swim.

Not me. On the first day I managed to stay in for an hour, paddling around mostly by myself. I was not as tough on the second (cooler) day, though; while I did go into the water, I spent 15 minutes treading water because actually swimming would have required me to repeatedly put my arms out of the water and back in. Too cold.

How cold? When a pre-teen step-grandnephew asked my three-year old grandniece if the water was cold, she replied, "No!" He dove in, came up sputtering and chattering to hear the rest of her response: "It's FREEZING!"

Just before heading out west for another family reunion (his side of the tree), I was invited to a friend's annual Pond Party. I have been to these events for the past 5 years but have never actually gone into the water. This year I was determined. I suited up and splashed right into the water, which was comfortably tepid. At the surface. Where the sun had been shining. A couple of feet below the top was a different story. I can't put an actual number on the temperature, but I can report that the only way to enjoy it was to float, and when the water was sufficiently stirred up and uniformly cold, I was glad that it was time to eat.

All of which should have prepared me for the family picnic in Spearfish, S.D., in the Black Hills. As soon as we arrived at the park, the kids dashed to the little river that runs through it. Following them, I was wishing that we had brought an old inner tube, since conditions were perfect for floating a few hundred feet downstream. Then I stepped into the water.

OHMIGAWD! Melting snowcap came to mind. Glaciers came to mind. Old Orchard Beach in April came to mind. By the time my ankles were wet, I couldn't feel me toes.

Luckily, it was time to eat.

Jeanne Bracken was bemused when a wiry fellow at the pool (who professed to swim like a rock) praised her effortless strokes. She guesses that this is one instance where a higher level of body fat is a Good Thing.

We Gotta Stop Meeting Like This

I have just returned from a family mini-reunion in Ohio and Pennsylvania. Ray and the girls had other commitments so didn't make the trip, which is why I basically spent four days in a moving vehicle with my mother, my sister and my brother. It's been a long time since we tried that one out, and it turned out surprisingly well. For most of us.

These reunions always have the potential for disaster. Not the family feud type, but for the most part medical ones. Actually, I don't think any of the factions are not speaking to any others, which is remarkable, considering that one cousin's current and previous wives were there.

Someone realized, about 20 years ago, that the only time we all got together any more was for weddings and funerals, and we were in something of a slump because the old-enough generation was pretty well married off (some more than once) and the older folks were holding their own, health-wise. We do tend to be long-lived; I think Grandma was 84 when she died, having survived a stroke several years earlier. Mom is an active 81 and three of her siblings made it well into their 80s.

So one of the cousins thought we should have a family reunion. She put it together and in 1983 a whole bunch of us turned up near Erie, Pennsylvania, for a weekend of fun and frolic. We had such a good time that other cousins planned reunions first every five years and then every three. We've been to West Virginia, upstate New York, Pennsylvania again, and New Hampshire.

Not that these reunions all went smoothly. At the first, the preschool son of the event-planning cousin fell and split his chin. A trip to the emergency room and stitches marked that reunion. The second reunion was more disastrous, with a ski-lift accident resulting in broken bones for three women. The upstate New York gathering didn't result in any hospitalizations but our motor home was laid up the whole time. We thought we'd broken the jinx with the Hershey reunion, but after the rest of the family left, Ray wound up with an abscessed tooth that required dental trips and serious drugs. Finally, the White Mountains weekend resulted in no hospitalizations, no illnesses, no dental emergencies, and no vehicular crises.

The next reunion won't happen for a year or two, but we have been gathering again for funerals. Aunt Lil died last winter but was so popular that there were three services for her—one in Maryland, her last home; one in Florida, her retirement home; and one in Ohio, where she raised her family.

The latter was postponed until spring so more relatives would be able to go. A cousin contacted area hotels to book a block of rooms. We were all instructed to ask for the Stanley Funeral Rate. Someone, making a reservation ahead of time, was asked by a plaintive clerk how on earth we knew so far in advance that someone would be having a funeral. Probably thought it was nervy of us, if we intended to bump someone off, to make such public plans.

It wasn't the whole clan that gathered, but there were a couple dozen of us. When we checked in at the hotel, the clerk said he was trying to put all the Stanley party on the same floor. I quietly observed to Mom that he didn't know us very well, did he? We really did behave for the most part. There was an afternoon pool party in which only two of the women went into the men's sauna. (Hey, the women's wasn't fired up!) There was a raucous dinner in the hotel dining room, which resulted in the waitstaff confusing us with the wedding party that was also in the hotel.

And someone did get sick. I'm not allowed to say who it was, so I will just call him "J"—which, trust me, is not a major clue in our family, since more than half of us have the initial "J." Instead of joining us for dinner, "J" and his wife went to the ER. We were not supposed to know what his problem was, although we were having a bit of trouble swallowing (sorry) the notion of an emergency tonsillectomy.

None of us can keep a secret worth a darn, so pretty soon everybody knew that "J" was suffering from a major hemorrhoid. "The size of Rhode Island," was one educated guess.

"J" survived his surgery and is recovering somewhere in another state. The rest of the family, meanwhile, is making him the butt of all the jokes.

Jeanne Bracken would never personally make fun of "J's" posterior problems. Not much.

2005 update: Mom is now an active 85-year-old and our most recent reunion was in California. Mollie got to drive on a California freeway, which seems to have been a Major Life Goal. Go figure.

In the Sight of God and This Congregation

Tales From the Nursery

It seemed innocuous at the time. They needed people to watch the children in the nursery during summer church services. Just one Sunday per family would do it.

Well, heck, I thought. It's certainly time for us to pitch in, and what with people on vacation, there shouldn't be more kids than Ray and I could handle. Besides, they wisely posted the sign-up sheet on a blistering hot Sunday when the basement nursery was a good 20 degrees cooler than the sanctuary.

So I signed us up.

By the time I realized that our Sunday would be one of those when another church in town would join us for services, it was too late to back out.

Oh well, it's just for an hour. What can happen?

Lots. As we found out on Sunday. We started off pretty well. I got some of those sticky name tags so we could keep track of the troops. As each child arrived, we stuck his or her name on the front of a shirt or dress. We even put a tag on Dorothy, who is Amanda's doll. One parent, wiser in the ways of the nursery than we, suggested that we put the smaller children's tags on their backs, and that made sense.

It didn't work, of course, but it was a nice try.

By the time the last child arrived (Nicholas), the others had all either swapped name tags or eaten them. There were a lot of children, too. I counted them several times but never got the same number twice. Mostly I noticed that, except for Lisa, they were all under the age of about four. And we were seriously outnumbered.

Ray counted and came up with 15, and I think he was pretty close with that. To make matters more interesting, at least three mothers told me, as they handed over their offspring, that it was really nap time but he or she will never sleep with all these kids here.

Ever the optimist, I still thought the two of us could handle it. But right about then Ray looked over the field, several of whom were crying, selected the smallest one, and parked in the rocking chair, where he stayed the first half hour. The second half hour he spent standing between two cribs amusing two no-longer-crying-infants.

Meanwhile, of course, I was dashing around after the other 13 or so youngsters. Lauren, who can't quite crawl yet, kept backing her legs under the toy shelves, and I had to rescue her. She also helped herself to Sarah's pacifier. Eventually I put her in a swing, where she survived the occasionally rough pushing of her sister and another darling little blonde (Jennifer? Sharon?) and even fell asleep. There was a free crib, but I left her in the swing; why mess with success?

Meanwhile, I had Sarah on one hip because whenever I put her down on the floor she would try to stand up and her sister (Jennifer? Sharon?) would try to help her "walk" across the floor, liberally strewn with toys, dolls, and small children. Sarah, bless her, stopped crying when I put her in the crib, probably because Ray was standing there amusing her. By then her name tag was on her elbow. I was appalled to note that she also had a bruise near one eye. I couldn't imagine how she had gotten it.

Margie, for no discernible reason, was wearing green sunglass and an "It's a girl" button. The identical twins were not dressed the same, but one had three name tags -- his own, Jennifer's and Sharon's and his brother only one, Amanda's. Luckily his mother had dressed Ben in blue, so I just had to remember that, by default, the other one was Nathan.

The absolutely worst one of the bunch, hands down was our Mollie. I have no idea if she acts that wild every

Sunday, but I will never again be able to drop her off at the nursery before church without feeling a certain amount of guilt. This kid alternately climbed up on her father's lap, pushed or pulled other kids around in a wagon, grabbed toys others were playing with quietly, and (I kid you not) climbed into cribs. This is Mollie, the kid who for the past few weeks has driven me crazy by climbing out of cribs when she was supposed to be napping. It wouldn't have mattered. I suppose, except that the kids who were already in the cribs weren't amused and would set up a howl when she plunked down next to them. She also had a name tag on the bottom of each shoe, Kyle's on one, Dorothy's on the other.

Fairly early in the hour, I noticed that the noise level had dropped considerably. Ah, things are quieting down. I thought. Danny had stopped crying. In fact...where was Danny? In the bathroom? Danny? The kid who once tried to vacuum a toilet? I dashed into the boys' room with Sarah on my left hip and Mollie hot on my heels. Found and removed Danny before he could get into any trouble.

Back out with the troops, I balanced Sarah on my left knee, read Kyle a Dr. Seuss book complete with page after page of sound effects, Amanda circling wide-eyed just out of my reach. Afterward, I noticed that one of the little ones needed a diaper change. But I couldn't figure out which one, and nobody would 'fess up. Everybody I checked was fine.

By the end of the hour Ray had taken on a definitely glassy-eyed look. Sarah's mother, retrieving her children, assured me that the bruise was there when they arrived and I wasn't responsible. I never did find out whose drawers needed changing.

And How Was <u>Your</u> Easter?

This year, I thought, Easter is going to be different. Organized. On time. Preparations finished before the Easter Bunny takes his first hop.

EASTER MINUS TWO WEEKS: We begin practicing some special choral music for church. Lisa has new shoes; I buy a pair for Mollie and put them out of reach so they'll stay white.

EASTER MINUS ONE WEEK: I pick out beautiful outfits for the girls. Choral rehearsals continue.

EASTER MINUS THREE DAYS: I go shopping for a few accessories for the girls and me. The store has no tights in either girl's size. I improvise, buying Lisa her first panty hose and Mollie white anklets, for which I buy some rainbow ruffles to jazz them up. I find purses to match each one's shoes. I buy two Easter baskets. Both are purple but one has a gold handle, to distinguish them. The girls fight over the one that's all purple. Drawing straws, Mollie wins it. Lisa sulks.

EASTER MINUS TWO DAYS: I put new buttons on Lisa's dress.

EASTER MINUS ONE DAY: We take the girls to their first-ever Easter egg hunt. Very interesting. A whirlwind of guess-how-many-jelly-beans-in-the-jars, decorating egg-hunting bags, scrambling for plastic eggs filled with chocolate surprises and stickers, and decorating cupcakes. Mollie guesses two jelly beans in the jar, and no amount of prompting will budge her to think of a higher number, any higher number.

Back home again, we perform the annual egg dyeing ritual. I boil a dozen eggs. One has a crack and the contents boil out all over the other eggs in disgusting shapes. As we dye them, most of the remaining eggs get cracked, but Mollie puts so many stickers on each one that Ray says they have new shells. Lisa and I put together the "train" that came with the egg dyeing kit; it takes all our skill and patience. Kids are supposed to do this themselves? I put the eggs in the refrigerator.

7:30 pm   I sew the ruffles on Mollie's socks. She hates them.

8:00 pm   We shampoo the girls. Hear that screaming? That's Mollie. She starts screaming half an hour before the water is drawn. It takes two of us to hold her down and do a quick wash. There is never a remote possibility that any of the baby shampoo will get in her eyes, you understand; so she makes up for that by screaming that there is water in her ears. We get her hair dried and put her to bed.

Hear that new screaming? That's Lisa getting her hair brushed out. She writes a lengthy note to the Easter Bunny, sets up the train with the dyed eggs and leaves him a glass of orange juice with a straw and a carrot, which she peels. We get her to bed. I put the eggs in the refrigerator.

9:00 pm   I hem my Easter dress.

11:05 pm   I finish mending my coat and putting new color-coordinated ribbons on my Truman Capote hat.

EASTER MORNING 5:05 am   Mollie appears at my bedside. "Mommy, I threw up," she cries.

5:06 am Lisa, awakened by the commotion, runs into the kitchen, then back yelling, "Mommy, look what the Easter Bunny brought!" She runs upstairs to show her father, who is not thrilled.

5:07 am I scoop jelly beans off the table and put them out of reach.

5:10 am Mollie, stomach apparently settled, demands breakfast. She eats a little, then plays with her offerings from the Easter Bunny.

5:20 am   I have retreated to the couch. Lisa, in the kitchen, falls off her chair.

5:25 am Lisa examines her basket and discovers that Mollie got a little bar of fancy soap and she didn't. "And I'm the one who collects soap," she moans. I tell her

I can't explain that. Another bar of soap eventually turns up on the floor. I return to the couch.

5:45 am I am invaded. "Let me sleep with you, Mommy," I hear, and I am sharing the couch with two kids, two dolls and one blanket. I abandon all hope of further sleep.

5:55 am Lisa gets dressed for church. Panty hose and all.

6:10 am Mollie gags some more and begins a croupy cough.

6:30 am Ray and I agree we have a problem. Mollie can't go to the church nursery and there is a fat chance she will sit still for two services while we take turns singing up front.

6:45 am We decide Ray will go to the early service. I will go to the second service. Lisa will go with me and sing in the junior choir debut. Mollie will not go at all. So much for the family that prays together. This decision upsets Mollie. She recovers quickly when she realizes she can wear her favorite purple corduroy pants. Thankfully, she has forgotten the new white patent leather shoes.

7:00 am Ray and I have breakfast: kielbasa, boiled eggs and toast. There are now 9 eggs left. I put them in the refrigerator.

7:15 am Lisa is asleep on the couch, shoes, purse and all.

7:30 am Ray leaves for the early service. Mollie brings me two Christmas books to read.

2005 update: Somewhere along the line Mollie learned to enjoy showers and shampoo. It is a happy day when her 45-minute morning shower leaves some hot water for anyone else. Lisa probably hasn't seen 5 am since 1985, and I go to church alone. Nobody sings in the choir.

Wild Thing

When I was a teenager, about a hundred years ago, there was a popular song that went "Wild thing, you make my heart sing. You make everything groovy." (The word "groovy" alone dates me.)

I think about that song now and then, mostly when I'm contemplating my younger daughter. She's barely three, but she's already a legend in her own time. Don't get me wrong – she's cute. Blue eyes, blonde hair, chubby cheeks. But behind that Baroque angel look lurks a child with a will of pure steel.

My little Wild Thing is going through a phase – at least I HOPE it's just a phase - where she hates everything. And everybody. And does not mince words in saying so. If I take her to places where children gather, she grabs all the toys for herself, then says to each other child, "I hate you."

Needless to say, this does not make her the most sought-after tyke in town. One memorable afternoon Mollie spent an entire two hour meeting telling Danny, "I hate you." Not surprisingly, Danny's feelings were hurt. When we got home, she confided, "I like Danny." I told her she had a funny way of showing it.

One morning we went to the supermarket and she told a neighbor we saw there, "I hate you." Loudly. The following week she saw the same neighbor again at the store maybe half a dozen times while we were making our rounds. In a better mood, I suppose, Mollie announced, "I like you." Over and over again. Whew!

She is still learning how to behave in church, too. This week the children had a worship service and someone must not have been paying attention, because Mollie found a place next to her buddy Danny. (A different Danny. She knows 3 kids by that name.) When the other children sat down, Mollie noticed that Danny had not taken a seat. She stood right there next to him and said, loudly, "Danny, sit down!"

Then there is the matter of clothes. I always heard that siblings aren't at all alike, and that is certainly true of Lisa and Mollie. Lisa is a fashion plate. She would prefer to wear silk and furs every day.

Mollie is to put it bluntly, a slob. She has one pair of purple corduroy slacks that she would gladly wear every single day. She has one pair of "Care Bear" pajamas that she would gladly wear every single night. She does not care for any socks except a certain kind of white ones, which are rapidly turning black from overuse and underwash. If she dresses herself when nobody is looking, it is guaranteed that someone (usually me) will have to force her to change into something decent or at least clean. She doesn't even mind digging the pants out of the dirty clothes hamper. This afternoon I noted with a sigh that at least the shirt was clean. Then she turned to walk away and I realized that she had taken the shirt out of the hamper, too, but she had it on backward so the dirt didn't show when she was facing me. Laying out any other outfit is asking for a tantrum, and I usually get one for my pains.

Frankly, for a long time I was able to convince myself that she was indeed just going through the terrible twos and would outgrow it. This despite the fact that the stage had begun when she was 18 months old and shows no sign of abating. Slowly it has dawned on me that this is her personality. What you see, as the saying goes, is what you get. For the next 20 years or more.

I suppose I can't lock her up in a tower somewhere for the duration. In the first place, houses don't have towers anymore. Besides, the law frowns on most of the things that fairy tale mothers did to keep their offspring in line.

I have discussed the problem with several friends, hoping that they will assure me that she will of course outgrow this. But every single one has said, with a shake of the head, that Mollie is always going to be a handful.

One friend had a solution. "Read this," she said, handing me James Dobson's "The Strong-Willed Child," "and know Mollie." Dobson, I have discovered, says a strong will is an asset in a child. That's easy for him to say. The strong-willed member of his family was a dachshund. And besides, he doesn't have to put Mollie in for a nap when she's not tired but I am.

Still, I'm willing to give it a shot. Okay, wild thing, I'm reading it.

But even as I read, I have a sinking feeling that someday Mollie will be writing a book of her own. About me. "The Strong-Willed Mother."

Oh well, it's better than "Mommie Dearest."

1989

Everything But Fleas

It doesn't seem to matter much what you call it. Flea market, lawn sale, yard sale, barn sale, garage sale, whatever—none of the names is very accurate. After all, you're not buying a lawn, a barn, a garage, a yard, or (you hope, anyway) a flea. I would have mentioned white elephants as well, but as it happened, our recent flea market table had not one but two white elephants on it.

This is all fresh in my mind because the church had a flea market last week. The array of goodies for sale would have warmed the cockles of a dump picker's heart. (I do not say this in judgment, because everyone knows that the flea market is the last stop before the local landfill. If nobody will pay a quarter for it, out it goes at the end of the day.)

There was a large, round, hemp decoration of some sort festooned with seashells. There were three carefully boxed meters, complete with directions and assorted accessories; unfortunately, none of us—not even the engineers—was able to figure out exactly what they measure. We had a pair of truly enormous Mediterranean-style wrought-iron table lamps. We had a make-up doll head complete with powdered paint and a pair of wigs, including a positively garish orange one. Lisa braided the blonde wig over it. It looked pretty presentable until the darling little girl with the folks at the next table painted the face completely blue.

We seized this golden opportunity to rid ourselves of some household dross. Things like a set of plastic snack trays with starburst flowers. A wine rack. A cedar nut basket that said "Lake Winnepesaukee." Several bottles of after-shave lotion that Ray didn't like. A lamp he bought at a yard sale a couple of years ago and we'd never even plugged in. (We got the same buck we paid, which

55

says something about inflation and depreciation, but I'm not sure exactly what.)

Of course, it is strictly against the law to attend a flea market in any capacity without buying something, so I was forced to take a few things home as well. In fact, the first phase of any flea market is the time set aside for those who are bringing in donations to buy things being brought in by others.

That's why I went home on Flea Market Eve with a bicycle, a set of canisters and a teapot for the camper. Ray pointed out, however, that the roasting pan I was eyeing probably wouldn't fit in the RV's cupboard, let alone its small oven.

I was delighted to find a small wok with a tempura rack. Both the pot and the rack will come in handy when I (frequently) stir-fry Chinese dishes or (occasionally) make tempura (deep-fried Japanese vegetables). The friend who donated the set from the back of her closet said she'd never used it, and besides, what the heck is tempura? An hour later another tempura set was donated by another puzzled person who wanted to know **what is tempura?**

Nor did it end there. On the day of the sale we arrived a few minutes before the official opening only to discover that people had been there shopping for over an hour. (Never announce the official hour your sale will start; name an hour or two later. People will come early and drive you crazy anyway, so fiddling with the hours will give you back an edge.)

Actually, the bike I bought for myself was one of a pair. Someone suggested that I buy the man's bike for Ray, but if I had even suggested it, he would still be laughing. As it was, the idea came to Ray himself the next morning, so both bikes are in our garage even as I write— which just goes to show that after 19 years there can still be some surprises.

The day of the sale I picked up a brand-new 1000 piece map puzzle of the US that looked easy but kept the youth group sitting as still as I've seen them all year. I also got a rope ladder that even matches her color scheme to use as an emergency exit from Lisa's new room.

As the hours passed, things got slightly cuckoo. Someone sold Mary's coat and was able to retrieve it just in the nick of time. Lois sold her money box and had to keep her proceeds in a plastic bag after that.

All in all, I thought we did pretty well. We were hauling home less than we had donated, which I considered a minor triumph. But that was before the "Final Hour", which at flea markets usually degenerates into a diabolical scheme to cheat the landfill called "Buck a Bag." The way this works is, the chump—I mean, customer—buys a bag for a buck and crams into it as much as possible of all the stuff nobody would even pay a dime for.

This seemed like a good idea until I discovered, too late, that Lisa was not flat broke after all, but still had a dollar. It's amazing what a simple grocery bag will hold without breaking. Syrup bottles, the glass lid to something, a plastic popsicle-making set (particularly galling since I had already mentally earmarked the popsicle set we have for the next sale.)

I'm already looking forward to the fall sale. I know exactly which cupboards I'm going to raid for discards. Because flea markets are fun—a bargain-hunter's paradise, a good fund-raiser, and a chance to clean up in more ways than one.

Everybody, in fact, benefits from a flea market.

With the possible exception of the mother who has to deal with the plastic popsicle-making set that has somehow come to rest in the back seat of the family car.

2005 update: The bicycles didn't get ridden much, the popsicle sets (both of them) are probably still in the cellar, and although we make tempura occasionally, we never used the flea market set.

Women, Unite on an Abbey Retreat

I have been to a number of camps and retreats before, but this one was different. For two days last weekend I was at an abbey in Harvard with about two dozen women from our church. Among us we left behind 40-some children and half as many husbands to spend time getting in touch without distractions. It was an amazing experience—a little like Girl Scout camp but without the snakes, bugs and tents.

We had a lot of fun and learned a lot, but I couldn't help thinking how different this experience was from what might happen on a similar men's retreat.

In the first place, it tends to be a lot more complicated for women to leave home for a couple of days. When guys are going away with their friends for the weekend, I'm willing to bet that most don't feel obligated to leave a big pan of lasagna or some other casserole lest their families starve while they're away—or live on take-out.

The women arrived at the abbey with clothing in real suitcases and other pieces of luggage, not (as I have seen men do) with their stuff in sports or duffel bags or what I refer to as Ray's "matched luggage"—brown paper sacks in various sizes. Women getting away from it all have something of a tendency to take everything with them; guys would not be sure to include entire boxes of tissues, for example, and in a guy group there probably would not be two dozen hair dryers.

Not being Catholic, I have never been to a monastery before; it was a real eye-opener. The Benedictines are a hospitality order, and after all these years they know what they're doing. Each of us had our own room, a real rarity for many, who haven't slept alone for decades. We were delighted to leave the snoring behind—until we discovered a) the walls are thin and b) yep, women snore. (No names.)

The retreat house had no telephones, no television. The word "impeachment" was not uttered once in 48 hours. The only bells were calls to vespers and other services, which were often said or sung in Latin; Gregorian chant lives! It was easy for us (many being mystery book lovers) to imagine Brother Cadfael in his robe and hood.

One of the nicest switches with a women's retreat at a monastery is that the men do the cooking (and are savvy enough to serve lots of chocolate desserts), and the women just show up for meals. Take that, guys!

Not that it's easy to get into a being-cared-for mindset. I can't picture a bunch of guys making sand pictures with driftwood and shells, or expressing their feelings with crayons (using non-dominant hand, please, to level the playing field for the non-talented among us.) But it sure was easy to believe the first comment when the sand pail was opened in the living room: "Who's gonna vacuum that up?" No guy would think of that.

It is beyond impossible to conjure up the image of a bunch of men giving each other hand massages with fragrant lotions. It isn't even easy to picture guys in pairs, small groups or the large gathering, everyone really talking about real stuff—"sharing", as the therapists call it. I plumbed more depths in two days of women's groups than Ray and I have covered in 29 years. At the end, someone commented that she hadn't laughed so much in ages, and I would agree.

Not only that, but none of the jokes were off-color or anything-ist.

Told to bring healthy snacks to a retreat, women arrive with boxes of clementines, ready-to-eat carrots, rice cakes, low-fat popcorn and the like. Guys think nachos made without the guacamole count as healthy, never mind the cheese, sour cream and chips. A steady supply of hot water suffices for women, many of whom drink tea, but I'd bet the guys would have held out for a coffee urn.

A monastery is no place for kids, which is part of the point. The lack of television would pose a real handicap for guys—no football? And besides, who would take charge of the remote control? Not a pretty sight.

The weekend weather left a lot to be desired, so outdoor time was a little limited, but we did get in some exercise between the raindrops. But nobody felt obliged to go jogging in the rain and mud. Guys would. Pairs of muddy shoes and boots were placed neatly beside the entry doors—not once did I trip over a pair of "gunboats" left lying in the middle of a room.

Since a woman planned the retreat, there were distinctly un-guy portions. For example, in the middle of the afternoon on Saturday, the schedule called for a two-hour nap. We didn't have to doze off in front of a television or have a newspaper (there weren't any anyway) fall on our faces to catch forty winks in the afternoon. I doubt guys would even think of that nap. (A couple of the women eschewed sleep for a quick shopping trip, which I also doubt the guys would have done.)

An open-ended "care and comfort" session concluded each day—not a bull (or cow) session but foot massages and impromptu discussions of good mystery books.

Two things, though, were most striking. A sign on the wall over the dining room sink said "Wash your own dishes." So we formed a line to wash, dry and put them away. Men would assume that the sign didn't apply to them (if they even read it to begin with) and would have piled the dishes in the sink. It wasn't until we'd finished the breakfast clean-up that we discovered that, indeed, the sign did not apply to us and the dishes should be— right!—stacked in the sink.

And, as one woman commented, not once was a toilet seat left up.

To join this man and this woman

1987

Home Again, or Back From the Brink

Vacation. The word packs almost as much high hope and expectation as the word "motherhood", and the realities are often about as humbling. While this year's vacation was not what I had originally planned, it turned out to be the stuff dreams are made of after all. Nightmares, to be exact.

When we changed our plans, we figured we'd make the best of things. We'd take four days to drive the more than 2000 miles to Denver. The theory was that, with the pickup and camper unit, the kids could sit in the back in comfort with a table for art or whatever, everybody would get a window seat, the dog would sit on the upholstered seat with the kids and not drool on me, I would not be able to hear them fight, and a fine time would be had by most.

You will probably not be surprised to hear that things didn't exactly work out that way. The first morning on the road, before we even got to Springfield, Mollie stuck her head through the communicating window between the cab and the camper, announced she had a tummy ache, and threw up on me. The dog spent about 1900 miles of the trip west standing in the camper with her head through that same communicating window. Drooling on me.

In Kansas we stayed at an Army Corps of Engineers Campground for a night. Nice place. Except that the "modern toilet and shower building" was...unusual. While the roof was the same size and shape as the building, it had been cleverly mounted so that all the corners of the room were exposed to nature. We never figured out

62

whether the Army did this in a whimsical mood or whether one of those Kansas tornados was responsible. This design is probably really swell on starlight nights, but in the rain it loses much of its charm. Gave a whole new meaning to the word "shower."

Nor did our adventures fail us when we reached our destination. There was Taco Bueno, Taco Bell, Taco This, Taco That—the kids started to look a little like nacho chips, so one day I said, "Let's have fried chicken."

It was the wrong thing to say.

Oh, the restaurant was clean enough, the service friendly and the food good. But the clientele were straight out of Monty Python. A guy trotted in carrying a sandwich, threw his duffel bag on the next table, took a seat next to me and started to talk. To me. "THE-WEATHER-ISN'T-IT-AWFUL-RAIN-CAN'T-EARN-ANY-MONEY," he said. Several times. Loud. Then "RAIN-CAN'T-EARN-ANY-MONEY-CAN-I-HAVE-A-FRENCH-FRY?"

They were Mollie's French fries. I said, "They're hers."

He subsided. I told Mollie through clenched teeth, "Eat those French fries."

The guy looked at my plate. "THERE'S-STILL-MEAT-ON-THOSE-CHICKEN-BONES-CAN-I-HAVE-THEM?"

"It's gone," I said.

"NO-THERE'S-STILL-MORE-MEAT-CAN-I-HAVE-THEM?" He still hadn't touched his sandwich.

"It's all gone," I said.

He reached over, grabbed the bones, chewed them to bits and threw the remainders back on my plate.

Where's Miss Manners when you need her?

Lisa complained about her ear of corn. Not sweet and fresh.

"Eat it," I said, fearing a rerun. The guy still hadn't touched his sandwich.

"Eat your French fries," I said to Mollie.

"Help me out here," I said to Ray. He ignored us all.

The guy's companion gathered him up and they carried their sandwiches out of the place. A woman at a nearby table said she didn't know whether to laugh or cry, then launched an unintelligible monologue about not even knowing what time it was. Loud. To me. We fled.

To an amusement park to recover. All four of the Brackens rode, for some reason, the roller coaster. Three of us kissed the ground upon landing. Mollie wanted to ride again. Ray said the Wild Chipmunk is better. "It's fun," he said. "Trust me," he said. I did. Fool. I emerged bruised and bleeding. Some fun.

The rest of the vacation was equally eventful. We met a bearded lady housekeeper with a battered wig, witnessed a mugging, and saw a near-miss in the not-so-friendly skies. It was time to head for home, but not before we acquired a family heirloom. Despite space and weight constraints in the camper, Ray accepted his cousin's accordion. I told him if he plays "Lady of Spain," that's grounds.

The accordion actually came in handy, making the trip east right behind the boot window between cab and camper, so the dog couldn't quite reach to drool on me.

The trip did have good moments, although not enough to balance the peculiarities the way I keep score. But as William Shakespeare said (or was it Joan Rivers?)—

There's no place like home, Toto.

2005 update: We also found out afterwards—long afterwards—that the kids had amused themselves by mooning passing vehicles through the window over the sink. So much for the extra expense of installing seat belts.

Locker Wars: Where Every Battle is a Losing One

We're slowly getting used to the middle school. Several weeks ago at "Back to School" night, the kids wrote out their schedules for us to follow, adding little personal notes on the back. Lisa just wrote: "Buy me some crayons." But one father read his son's warning: "Don't look in my locker."

That was probably the first time I had given any thought to Lisa's having a locker, too, and if I'd known the number, I would have brought home her raincoat—the one she took to school about the second day and I hadn't seen since. The one I suggested every day that she bring home because it was bound to rain some morning. That raincoat.

Still, I did pretty well on "Back to School" night from the school's lost-and-found—a very familiar sweater, scarf, knit hat, and jacket—the basics of Lisa's fall outerwear. I came home a changed woman, for it had finally sunk in that last year's Clean Desk Battle had escalated into The Locker War.

This innocuous few cubic feet of non-locking steel-encased independence has now surpassed the family dog and even the little sister as The Excuse.

As in: "Where are the new crayons your father bought you?"

"Someone stole them from my locker."

Or: "Where is your hat/mitten/notebook/raincoat?"

"In my locker."

Another day: "If you don't have any homework, how come you lugged home seven textbooks, a notebook and two workbooks?"

"I didn't want to go back to my locker to put them away."

And frankly, I would have been surprised if they fit, because I have Been Enlightened, by proxy. I sent her father to the school one afternoon to bring back the better part of Lisa's wardrobe and some of her sister's. He was also supposed to look for some overdue library books.

Little did I know that his pickup truck would be barely adequate for the task. The pair dragged home several bags of miscellany.

"What on earth is this?" I demanded.

"That's the stuff out of my locker."

A pair of snow pants, two raincoats, textbooks, papers, sneakers, soap, a mildewed towel and washcloth, three shirts, four sweaters, a gym suit, hat, scarf, mittens and a moldy peanut butter and jelly sandwich (I think).

I was transfixed by the collection, but some of us are never satisfied. "What, no library books?"

"Nope," he reported.

The very next day, I heard, Lisa's locker was declared a disaster area. She couldn't open it at all.

"All the books and notebooks sort of fell," she reported, "and I couldn't get it open. Neither could the teacher. She sent for help."

But as it turned out, reinforcements weren't necessary. Another fifth grader, obviously more savvy, got Lisa's locker open using muscle, know-how, and a single well-placed kick.

"And guess what!" she added. "I found the overdue library book on the shelf in my locker."

Her father, confronted with that irrefutable evidence of incompetence, was fired on the spot as Designated Locker Cleaner. "I got MOST of it," was his excuse—apparently the bottom MOST, and my best guess is that Lisa is the shortest kid in the history of the middle school and probably needs a ladder to see what's on that top shelf of the locker. Heaven only knows how she gets the stuff up there to begin with.

By then intrigued, I asked Lisa what else was in her locker that her father hadn't fetched. "Oh, some pens, some long-lost homework, loose change, a broken social studies project, some more old lunches...maybe a few mice, rats, spiders..."

I wouldn't doubt it. Of course, none of this surprises me. After all, what we have in that locker is her room in microcosm. They should have another category on the report cards: Locker Stuffing. She'd get an A. The kid has a real future canning sardines, packing parachutes, or folding road maps.

In the meantime, I have had my consciousness raised. I thought catching the bus would be a big hassle this year, but Lisa has done really well. In fact, she's only missed it twice—once in the morning and once, I got a call at work.

"Mom," she said, "I'm at school. I missed the bus."

"How'd that happen?" I wanted to know.

"Well, you told me to bring my raincoat home. But when I went back to my locker to get it, the bus left without me."

If anybody can figure out the proper response to that one, I'd love to hear it.

An Ill Wind Blows

I'm typing this as fast as I can because I want to finish it before the power goes out. Also, of course, I want to skip town, but that will have to wait for a while longer. What I'm talking about here is the Vacation from Hell.

I should have known months ago not to expect much. I had applied in early spring for the last two weeks in August, only to discover that the time was already taken by a co-worker and I'd have to stick around to work. Eventually, through a set of circumstances too involved to get into, that situation resolved itself (without, I assure you, the assistance of a hit person) and we were again looking at two weeks in August in central Massachusetts at a quiet campground. It wasn't going to be perfect, but with some interesting day trips, it had real potential.

I collected books for every member of the family (UFO books for Ray, ghost books for Mollie, horror books for Lisa, beside which my historic novels and armchair travel selections look positively normal) and phoned for information about various amusement parks and water slides in two states. My last day of work was Thursday, and we spent Friday getting our act together – we thought. I tried not to obsess about the two "minor" fires Ray had somehow triggered in the RV, or the dead battery. Why? I wanted to know: it will be fine, he reassured me.

I just kept packing and making lists. Saturday we picked Lisa up at camp, secure in the conviction that for once we would get her and she would be healthy. Her usual pattern has been to
start throwing up about 10 minutes after we get her, but we were sure that her recent operations had settled all that. We were on the road by 7 a.m. (so far, not much rest on this vacation, but it would come, right?), picked Lisa up a little after 9 and headed Down East.

We were fine until lunch time, which found us at the famous Moody's Diner in Waldoboro. We ordered. Lisa started to look a little odd. I have cramps, she said. There was a line at the bathroom: it didn't bode well for the three-hour drive ahead of us. Suffice it to say, we stuck to scenic and traffic-jammed Route 1 for much of the trip home; by Freeport, she was feeling fine and we hit for the interstate in relief.

We had planned to leave on Monday. Saturday evening Ray announced that the RV wouldn't start, then came back a little while later to say he'd lied and everything was fine. Sunday we finished packing, took the cat to "Aunt" Gloria's, and got into the car. The RV wouldn't start. That was yesterday, and it still hasn't, although apparently we're on the brink here.

Luckily, I'm not on the brink myself. I have been able to discern a brighter side to all this. Take Lisa's eye. If we had gone camping on Sunday as planned, we would have been a long way from help if she had been reading the newspaper at the campground and all of a sudden felt something in her eye. As it was, the trip to the emergency room to have a splinter removed from the inside of her right eyelid wasn't nearly as dramatic as it could have been.

So Monday morning in the rain Ray went to seek more help with the RV problem and I schlepped out to get the newspaper that the delivery service assured me will be the last delivered for the next two weeks. And opened the paper. And discovered for the first time that this was no line of showers but a Genuine Hurricane Bob at our doorstep.

Oh well, I thought, I can still run errands. Except the bank was closed and the library was, too. I bought rabbit food, but in the process nearly lost my keys and forgot where I put the rabbit treats I bought for Dulcie, who is already at "Aunt" Lisa's in Leominster for her two-

Someday We'll Laugh About This

week hiatus from the Bracken House of Insanity (as Mollie answers the phone).

So maybe we'll get to the campground on Tuesday. We do have to come back for an appointment on Wednesday, but maybe after that we can go sit by the pool for whatever is left of our two weeks. Reading about UFO's and ghosts and horrors and star-crossed millworkers named Sabra and Emmeline.

One thing that didn't get done in the first wave of vacation planning was this column, which I figured I'd write and deliver from the woods before the deadline. The storm is intensifying and I hear sirens, but at least the power is ...ZZZZZT.

Taking Leave of Town—and Our Senses

I cannot begin to describe the highlights of Our Summer Vacation without one last hurricane story. This is for the light crew that fixed whatever blew on the light pole outside our living room window late the Monday night of "Bob." In the process of extinguishing all lighting materials, I dropped a lamp and the glass chimney shattered. I immediately got the vacuum cleaner for the glass. But in case the light crew heard me, I do not want to go down in Hurricane Bob history as the lady who sat around her darkened house waiting to vacuum at 10 p.m. I ain't that kinda girl!

Anyway, once we finally got past the hurricane, we did get to skip town. We visited not one but two amusement parks *plus* a water slide. In order to go to the latter, we had to drop the dog at a kennel for a day. Ray located one and called; sure, bring her on over, they said. Ray got back into the car and started to drive.

Where is it? I asked him.

Just down the road, he assured me.

How far? I asked him.

Uh...he replied.

What's the name of it? I asked him.

Uh...he replied.

What town is in in? I asked him.

Uh... it starts with P...he replied.

What does? The town or the kennel? I asked him.

Uh...he explained, while I made some very rude, unrepeatable comments about men's inability to ask for directions. Let's just say my commentary involved anatomically suggestive possibilities.

Fortunately, he swallowed his pride and asked directions just a mile or so from the kennel. We never would have known how close we were if he hadn't asked, though, because the kennel's sign (both the town and the kennel started with P. incidentally) had been knocked down by a garbage truck and we would have found the place about Columbus Day. 1992.

So we dropped the dog at the kennel and headed for the water slides, where we actually had a pleasant time until in a moment of weakness I agreed to tackle the 4,000-foot alpine slide with Lisa. The trip down was perfectly all right, even fun. But the trip up the mountain involved a chair lift. Mega white knuckles time. When we reached the summit and followed the painted footsteps out of the line of fire of the swinging chairs, I commented to Lisa that they should have a big set of lips painted on the deck, too, to show where to kiss the ground.

At the amusement park later that week, Ray emerged from the Round-Up looking a little green around the gills. I felt somewhat smug that I knew better than to tackle that, but I was instead sucked in by a serious alien force that dragged me on the swings, where I flew around on flimsy chairs at heights greater than the tallest redwood tree, for approximately (I'm guessing here) 43 days.

On the caterpillar ride (which is a small, covered roller coaster) Ray and I sat together and I think he was trying to get frisky, but I'm still not sure what he had in mind considering the centrifugal force we were experiencing at the time. We waited in line for several weeks to ride a simulated log flume, which not only dropped your lunch into your toes but got your clothes soaked in the process. Lisa wanted to experience a latter-day Spanish Inquisition (read: chair lift); she went alone.

The "fun house" (a euphemism if I ever heard one) sounded pretty tame. Little did I know that the experience would culminate in a "barrel walk." This looked harmless until I discovered it had been designed by an engineer who had consumed a case of Jack Daniels. Sober persons such as myself were not built to walk inside rolling surfaces. I came to this realization when I was on my knees — no, my backside — no, my shoulders...and learned the origin of the expression "I've fallen and I can't get up."

When my floundering around on the floor became a nuisance for the crowds piling up behind me, and when Ray was unable to extricate me, and when I knocked the kids over, the attendant (eyes glazed from listening to Julie Andrews sing "A spoonful of sugar" for several hours at a time) stopped the thing so I could escape. The bruises will be gone by Christmas. Probably.

The amusement park experience culminated in a ride on the Ferris Wheel. This actually looked okay to me, since the cars were partly enclosed and the paint on the superstructure didn't seem to be peeling, so I figured it was safe enough. However, as soon as we had lift-off, even before our car was stopped at the top of the wheel for an entire semester of calculus, Ray got this funny look in his eyes. The wheel went around maybe four or five times, six tops, although Ray swears it was at least 100. I wouldn't know, because I spend the entire time speaking very calmly to Ray and making eye contact so he wouldn't notice that our car in the parking lot below looked like a model from Matchbox.

So if you go on that particular Ferris Wheel and wonder about the lip marks at the exit marked "kiss the ground here," you can thank Ray, because he put them there.

Jeanne Bracken loves that tilt-a-whirl.

1994

Freezer Burned

I always say timing is everything. We had been postponing a semiannual food delivery until the freezer was empty so we could defrost it before loading the new stuff. Then we set a date. Thursday.

I told the delivery people that they had to come after 2:30 p.m. so Ray could deal with the hassle. Little did I know! We also thought that the timing was good because Mollie had invited a bunch of friends over for the weekend, and we could feed them some of the pizza that would come with the order.

On the day before the order, the delivery people called to confirm the time. Yes, they'd come after 2:30 p.m. No problem. Then on Wednesday night Ray went down to empty the last of the food and bring it up to the kitchen freezer.

"Um, he said, "not all of this is frozen..."

"What? I came back, brilliantly, heart sinking.

"Well, most of it is frozen, but some of it...isn't"

I cross-examined him and determined that the stuff that was frozen had been piled together at one side of the freezer, and the stuff that was not frozen had been isolated on the other side.

You know how all the manuals say to keep the freezer full for the most efficient operation? I was sure that was the problem (chalk it up to the later hour; my brain goes off-duty from household disasters at 8 p.m.)

Just to confirm my diagnosis, I called the Big Department Store appliance department. Their repair people had gone home hours before, but the sales person thought I should have a chat with them. They open, he added, at 7 a.m.

OK. We got some sleep and in the morning I wiped out the freezer and turned it back on. It got cold. Well, some places got cold and others got cool. At 7 a.m. I was on the phone to the department store repair people.

Sounds like someone should look at it, the lady said.

So, I called the delivery people to postpone the order. The cheerful recording announced that my call would be welcome after 9 a.m. — by which time I figured the truck would be on the way.

I called the appliance repair people, who agreed that the situation deserved a look-see and it sounded like the freezer might be low on Freon. They could come sometime in the early afternoon. They agreed to call Ray at work before heading to the house. Meanwhile, my friend Angela said there was plenty of room in her freezer and we could send the truck there to deliver it temporarily — but not 'til after 3 p.m. The timing, as I say, is everything.

I called Ray at work, dumped it all on him, and went to work myself.

The next I heard was about noon, when Lisa called from home and said the local repair person wanted to talk to me.

"Isn't your father there?" I asked.

"Nope. The repair guy just showed up and I had to get up and I'm not really even dressed," she said. Timing.

The repair guy, Lisa told me afterward, had felt all around in the freezer and causally asked, "Had this a long time?"

"Yes," said Lisa.

"Good," said the repair guy.

What he meant was, "Did you get your money's worth out of this now-dead appliance?" And then he gave it last rites. Lisa did say that her father had postponed the food delivery for a couple of weeks, just in case.

Just in case, indeed. Regular readers will remember that the weekend that Mollie's friends came over also turned into the weekend that Lisa ended up in the hospital. Timing. This was all happening simultaneously.

On Friday, after checking various consumer publications for repair records and debating whether to go for a slightly smaller unit, we finally settled on a particular model (slightly bigger than the old one) and on Friday night, Ray ordered it by phone, since the sale was over on Saturday and we knew, with Ray working and a houseful of girls, nobody would be able to go back to the store in person — and that was before Lisa's temperature shot up higher than the dead freezer.

The freezer pickup was on hold until Mollie's friends left and by then Lisa was back in the hospital for the second time that weekend. Which is why Ray called me at the hospital and asked if I wanted to go with him to pick it up.

"No," I said, and then I asked, "Who is going to help you carry it into the house?"

"Mollie" he said, and I had two quick thoughts. First, I'm sorry I won't be a fly on the wall to see *that one*. And second, What *is* it with guys that they can't ask anybody for help?

I got home late that evening and found Ray in the kitchen with the new freezer.

"Need help getting it downstairs?" I asked.

"Doesn't fit."

We had carefully assessed everything about the unit except its outside dimensions. There are only two doors in our entire house that it will go through (if you count the garage as part of the house...), and neither of them goes to the cellar. And, he added, it only went in the front way when he took the door off the hinges.

Which is why we now have a freezer in the kitchen, wrecking my carefully planned renovations but at least handy. And working.

And the food order is now due in two days. We're planning on having pizza for dinner on Saturday. Timing is everything.

Shop... Until Someone Drops

In these days of blending gender roles, it has probably come to your attention that His Chores and Her Chores are no longer clearly defined as they were in the days, say, of cave-dwelling. Way back then, he killed it, she cooked it, they ate it, end of story. Today, however, in the first place most of us don't have to kill our dinners—although my "make mine well-done" husband has on occasion complained that his steak so rare there was some question it was already deceased.

Still, the days of Donna Reed and "Father Knows Best" are long gone. Women are running snow blowers and changing oil in the family chariots, acting as financial planner and accountant. Men are cooking and sometimes even cleaning up after themselves, doing laundry and schlepping kids around. So when we went through one of our "let's split the chores more evenly" phases a few years ago, one duty that I was pleased to forego was the weekly grocery shopping.

This has its good moments and its bad moments. The good ones are when he goes to the store and I don't. The bad ones are when he comes home and I realize he's spent twice what we budgeted but still didn't get half the stuff on the list.

I griped about it but wasn't willing to rethink the venture. When it became obvious that leaving Ray in charge of grocery shopping meant we would be living on hamburger and canned green beans, we signed on with a food service that comes twice a year with stuff like chicken and fish, cauliflower and spinach. And every now and then I'd join Ray on his weekly forays into Supermarketland. Couples need quality time, right?

Well, not exactly. You know those happy couples on television ads, cheerfully discussing purchases from paper plates to sports cars, with little dissention and a lot of mutual respect? Those ads lie; they should carry the disclaimer: "These shoppers are professionals. Do not attempt this yourself."

Our joint shopping trips were invariable disasters, in which we'd spend four times the budget and have trouble fitting everything into the refrigerator.

Not only that, but while we were shopping "together", we'd hardly see each other from the time we entered the store until we chanced upon each other at the checkout stand a couple of days later.

Part of the problem was the timing. You know how you're not supposed to shop when you're hungry? Good advice, but I'd add, never shop when you're tired. Now since I am tired roughly 99.9% of the time, being Woman Who Has It All, there are clearly few windows of opportunity for me to shop when I'm at my best.

As a result, when Ray and I go to the Giant Warehouse, he gets a cart and we start up and down the aisles, which resemble runways for 747s. He stops at each food demonstrator's table, has a sample, chats, thinks about a purchase, and spends a few minutes figuring out where the product is shelved. Meanwhile, I'm dashing up and down the aisles, several weeks ahead of him, selecting what's on the list and ignoring most of the rest of the stuff. So while he's schmoozing with the burger lady or sidetracked by a display of socks, I'm staggering under a case of soup with a can of frozen orange juice in each armpit, wondering where on earth he's gone.

Obviously, for the sake of our marriage, we don't do this very often. But our microwave oven had died, and after a suitable period of mourning, we had decided to replace it. We didn't need a big one. Just one of the small ones, since we mostly make tea, reheat things and "bake" potatoes. We shopped around. We priced the microwave ovens at the first place. I took copious notes: Model number, features, size, price...

We bought a whole lot of groceries (as well as garden tools, little tables for the porch, plant food, huge plastic tumblers for summer drinks, our first-ever electric can opener...) and packed the stuff into the car. At the second Giant Place, we bought a few more groceries and compared the microwaves. The models were of course similar. Sure enough, there was a small one that would suit our purposes fine. But the wattage...For just $10 more would get.... And the size...For just $11 more than that...

In the end the comparison shopping came down to one model that was available at both Giant Places. The price was the same, to the penny.

After all that discussion, we realized we had settled on exactly the same microwave model we already had— although to give the Giant Places their due, we had spent 20% less than the last time, when it was on sale at a Famous Supposedly Discount Department Store.

By then we had a heck of a time fitting it into the car, but I was so tired that I would have willingly given the microwave my seat and tied myself to the roof, if only it meant we could finally go home.

That was several weeks ago, and I haven't set foot in a supermarket since. Every week we look in the pantry and freezer, decide we really don't need anything but milk and bread, and Ray goes to the store and comes home with eight brown bags of crackers, salad dressing and taco sauce. And I whine a little, and then, in the time honored wifely way, like the cave dwelling woman whose husband brought home mastodon instead of ichthyosaur, I kiss him and help him put the stuff away.

Then I go back to trying to figure out how the electric can opener works.

2005 update: The food service is history, we still spend too much on groceries, and the can opener has gone to the dump, never having been used to sharpen a knife, seal a bag, or open very many packages. We have a whole new can opener to hate.

Clouds Really Have a Silver Lining

By the time you read this (Lord willin' and the creek don't rise), Ray and I will have celebrated another Wedding anniversary.

It's a biggie, too; the 25th. What this means is that I have now been married longer than I was single. Now I was sort of a late bloomer, not getting hitched until I had almost finished grad school, so achieving 25 years of marriage is not really anything to write home about. Heck, lots of people today are married 25 years or more. But Ray and I have racked up that quarter of a century in only one marriage.

This is, in my family of origin, a record. I think it's even a record if you add up all of my siblings' marriages. We have a long way to go, however, to set a Bracken record; his parents were married 54 years.

Naturally, you are asking yourself, how did they do it?

Darned if I know. If you go by the experts, we did everything wrong. Many of our friends lived together before marriage; we didn't even live together for the first year afterward. We married in haste without even the proverbial shotgun as an excuse: we had known each other less than a year, got engaged after dating for just four months, and most of that time he spent at sea. After the wedding, we were separated more than we were together for the first several years. And we faced serious illness of a child, which should have been the final blow.

Our interests are so different that "opposites attract" does not begin to cover it. Ray was raised in the city; I am a country girl. He drinks coffee; I live on tea. He prefers a rum and Coke when we're ordering (to go with his burger and fries), I always ask for white zinfandel (to accompany my salad bar). He was born in Nebraska, I in New York. He was raised southwestern, I'm a Yankee through and through. His wild oats were sown in the Orient (courtesy of Uncle Sam), mine in Europe (thanks to Higher

Education). He selects the oldies radio station while I alternate between country and classical (depending on the time of day and the state of traffic). We were both raised by church-going families, but mine is a pretty liberal Congregationalist bunch and his were pretty conservative Lutherans.

He reads sci-fi, I read mystery. He gets his news from Channel 5 and ABC, mine comes via the *Boston Globe* and *People Weekly*. I studied liberal arts and languages; Ray was in a seminary. I put myself through college and grad school; he dropped out of college after one spectacularly bad (and as I hear it, riotous) semester.

I went to school in New Hampshire; he went to school in Texas. I was raised on stuff like lasagna, which I cooked myself; he was raised on chicken-fried steak, and the only thing he knew how to cook when I married him was "bachelor slop."

(Recipe: mix together one can of tuna and a can of the soup of your choice; don't bother heating them, but put them over hot instant rice, stir and enjoy. Come to think of it, he probably married me to get away from a lifetime of "bachelor slop." If microwave ovens had been invented 25 years ago, we might still be single).

I "surf the 'net" and browse on the World Wide Web; he has never figured out his CB radio.

The differences go back beyond the current generation. My father was in high tech as early as World War II; his father was a boilermaker for the railroads, a dying industry. My mother has an associate degree; his went only to the third grade. My step-grandfather sold ice in New York City; his cooked for the cavalry when they still rode horses.

Somehow, though, we have managed to overcome those differences- or at least keep them interesting. We have survived eight cars, three moves, one house purchase, one major home renovation project that will never be finished in this lifetime, eleven jobs, the deaths of two parents (adoptive) and one parent (step), three recreational vehicles of escalating cost and hassle factor, two dogs, four cats, two rabbits, two hamsters, at least six or eight fish, four computers, four mortgages, five home equity loans, two daughters, and yes, three microwave ovens.

We have quit smoking together--twice. We have lost and gained hundreds of pounds, gone from single lens to bifocal glasses, survived many operations (mostly Lisa's but also Ray's hernia), one 911 call, and one house-filled-with-smoke-night when we should have called 911.

Twenty five years ago I had hair down my back and Ray had more on his head than on his face. He also had way more teeth. The silver of this anniversary, trust me, is "silver threads among the gold." We have gone from paying off my college loans to applying for Lisa's.

Some marriages die but nobody has the courage to pull the plug. I don't think that's the case here. But if you were to pin me down, I'd have to admit that the cottage is covered with ivy of the poison variety, the love boat is a leaky inflatable raft, and we're both rowing as fast as we can, although in opposite directions, so we're just going around in circles.

And as we row, we sing "our song": "Debt, debt will keep us together. Think of that babe, whenever some sweet talkin' dude comes along."

2004 update: more cars, more home "improvements", more cats, two more microwave ovens, Mollie in college...same old, same old.

To live together

Kindergarten: So far, So Good

People have been asking us about kindergarten. Does Lisa like it? She sure does, which didn't surprise me much, considering how eager she is to get out of the house whenever possible.

It's been an interesting experience for all of us, although I do not look forward to another 12 years of struggles getting her out of bed in the morning. I've dealt with the problem so far by putting her to bed earlier and earlier. The way I see it, by the time she's a senior, she'll have to go to bed half an hour before she gets home.

The other day I asked Lisa what her class had done in art that day.

"We painted covers for our portfolios, but we can't take them home 'til the end of the year."

'Portfolios?' I thought. I was suitably impressed. Not bad for a five-year-old. We must have quite a school there.

Then:

"Mommy?"

"Ummm?"

"What's a portfolio?"

That's more like it. But that wasn't the only big word she learned.

They have been having visits in her classroom from some special "people": the letters of the alphabet. So far they have seen, among others, Mr. M (who found M&Ms in some odd places) and Mr. T (which led to Tootsie Rolls between someone's toes.)

The letter home explaining the program suggests that we talk each week about what words start with that week's letter.

She was pretty good when we tried that, so I thought I'd throw her a letter they hadn't had yet. "What starts with 'L'?" I asked.

"Lisa!"

"Yes, and what else?"

She thought for a brief moment.

"Elementary!" We laughed, then I praised her and apologized for the English language.

"Try again."

"Um, what's that long word? Laryngitis!"

I decided the game had gone far enough when I had to get out a dictionary to figure out how to spell the words she'd learned in kindergarten.

Despite all the safeguards, check and balances to prevent such an event, Lisa managed one day to get on the wrong bus. Naturally, it was a day when there was a substitute driver who didn't realize she had a problem sitting back there.

Lisa reported later, through tears that had apparently gained in intensity for a couple of miles, that she pointed out her house to the driver, "but immediately she turned the wrong way!"

Obviously the driver didn't hear her. Fortunately, the car was all warmed up and I caught up with them in a few minutes. It didn't speak well of her opinion of me as a mother that she thought I would leave her there.

What did she think I would do? Like Charlie on the MTA, pass her a peanut butter and jelly sandwich every morning as the bus turned the corner at East Roxbury Drive?

I certainly harbor no ill feelings that the incident happened, and I am secure in the knowledge that from now on the teachers will be watching Lisa like a hawk when she gets on a bus. I also know from conversations that similar things have happened in the past to others, and in some instances to whole groups of kids at the same time. Judging by Lisa's reaction, I pity the drivers who end up with two or three wailing kids. Just one more reason why bus drivers deserve combat pay.

But my favorite kindergarten story is this:

School had been going on for a couple of weeks when I finally heard what happened in the classroom on the first day.

Lisa announced casually one afternoon, "Betty's friend Nick works at my school."

"Nick? Nick who?" I was puzzled.

"I don't know his other name but he came to our room. You know, Betty's friend Nick."

"Honey, I don't know who you mean."

"You know, Mrs. D's friend Nick."

Suddenly, horrifyingly, the light dawned. "Do you mean Dick?"

"Yea, Mrs. D's friend."

"Uh, did you talk to him?"

"Yes, I called him. 'Dick! Dick!' and he answered me.

So that's how I found out that on the first day of kindergarten, in front of the whole class, Lisa called the superintendent by his first name.

Blood on the Badge

It's June. I know this not because I have turned all the calendars in the house (although, for once, I have), nor because the poison ivy is back, nor even because Lisa is counting the days until school is out (she's been counting since April.) I know it's June because every night of the week there are banquets, parties, award ceremonies, concerts, all those things that say, loudly, End of The Year.

Specifically, I knew it was June because I started getting notices about the annual Girl Scout Court of Honor. The leaders know me pretty well; they start sending me these notices several weeks ahead of time. With each one, I make a mental note: Do Something About Lisa's Uniform.

Last year I sewed all the badges onto her Brownie uniform about 13 hours before the ceremony where she became a Girl Scout (read: new uniform). Then I snipped them all off and recycled the uniform with the younger girls in town.

Lisa was given a green jumper that, worn with a white blouse and green socks, has passed nicely when she needed a uniform. As to the insignia, I had intended all along to go buy a sash for all that gear, reasoning that it would fit for years.

I figured I could sew the missing button back on the jumper, fix the sash, and I'd be set for a while. Just 25 hours before the ceremony, I sent Ray and Lisa to the store to buy the sash. The store was out of sashes. The lady said we could get one in a few days when they restocked. We didn't have a few days.

So we settled for a vest in the smallest size and, to top off the whole outfit jauntily, a green beret. Late that evening, when I got home from work, I bit the bullet (and also the thread) and got all the gear together to sew the insignia onto the vest. A little tag that came with the vest showed where the various pins and badges should be placed. The picture was tinier than Halley's comet, and some of the items we had weren't on it.

Ray was a big help. He kept offering advice on where the insignia had to be placed on his old Coast Guard Uniforms.

Thanks a lot, I said, mentally heaving a sigh of relief that I didn't have those to sew anymore.

I'm going to wing it, I said to myself (my spouse by then having gone to bed). I laid out all the stuff and decided where to put them. Then I started in. It wasn't easy. Despite my 20 years of embroidery experience, from samplers to elaborate counted cross-stitch ornaments and decorations, the badges looked like they had been sewed on by a person who never held a needle before and who had both arms in casts.

These badges are made to last. They are very stiff. No normal human being can put a needle through them. The Incredible Hulk would have trouble. Besides, someone had made off with most of my sewing needles and I was reduced to using one that Mother would call a crowbar. I managed to drill that sucker half an inch into my thumb, blunt end first, before I got smart and used a thimble. In the meantime, however, I bled a lot. There is one emblem in particular that I have come to call my Red Badge of Courage.

I thought I was doing okay, all things considered, until I came to the troop numerals. Last year I complained because the troop number had three digits. This year there were only two. A 9 and a 3. Or were they a 6 and a 3? Was it Troop 39? 36? 63? Whom can you call at 12:30 am to ask? I went with my first instinct, 93. Luckily.

Right about there I remembered a mother telling me last year that, in an emergency, she stapled the badges on. I tried that. Frankly, it looked awful. Maybe she meant that staples would hold them in place until they could be sewed; if so, she was right. I finally figured out how to stitch them so they not only were firmly in place, but they looked good, too.

I finished the last few in the morning. There, I thought, putting the vest with the jumper (missing button replaced), a pair of matching green socks, a white blouse, and the new beret.

I'd like to tell you that Lisa looked great in the uniform. I'd like to tell you the awards ceremony was a highlight of our year. I'd like to tell you we went out into the storm to watch this year's crop of Brownies "fly up" into Girl Scouts (and new uniforms.) I'd be lying.

Approximately two hours after I finished the uniform, Lisa came down with chicken pox.

2005 update: Lisa didn't stay in Scouts long enough to outgrow the vest. But she must have learned something, because she has developed an interest in quilting.

Showered With Surprises

Sometimes I wonder about us. I wonder why we keep going away for these vacations, given what usually happens along the way. Take our spring vacation. Not only did we have some colorful automotive problems, as you have read in this space, but there were a couple of unnerving incidents that had absolutely nothing to do with the fact that we were roaming the countryside in an antique recreation vehicle.

As usual, it had to do with the showers. I'm fussy about my showers. A shower away from home tends to be disappointing. At best. Either I have to plaster myself against a metal wall to avoid drowning, or the water just drips from the showerhead without any force at all, or the water is cold, or the water is hot and turns cold at blinding speed, then turns scalding. Not a lot of fun.

So I wasn't surprised when, showering in a Virginia campground, I had a couple of shocks. The temperature was okay. So was the showerhead. It was the company that caused the problem. First off, there was the security guard. The guard was not of the female persuasion. Luckily, we discovered each other verbally rather than visually. The real heart-stopper was the Close Encounter of the Amphibian Kind. I was enjoying the shower until, turning, I found myself face-to-face with a translucent green frog that was clinging to the shower curtain at eye level. I don't know which of us was more startled, but I know who yelled loudest. I don't know where the frog went, either, but it only took two leaps to disappear, and for the rest of our vacation, I approached the showers with a stick to beat the curtain before entering.

That was several weeks ago, long enough that I have mellowed about it. Which is why we not only went camping last weekend, but we did an Experiment. We took a friend along. I didn't know her well, but she and Lisa get along, and right up until her mother told me the kid doesn't like trees, I was sure we'd done the right thing. Hoo boy, I thought.

But it turned out okay. For the most part. Once we got settled. Setting up camp isn't our finest hour, and this time was no exception, as we moved from site to site trying to get the RV level so the refrigerator would work. While Ray (mostly) and I struggled with that, the kids were setting up the tent. No matter how much Ray (mostly) and I tried, we couldn't get the front of the RV high enough or the back of the RV low enough.

So we moved from one section of the campground to the other, pursued by a hoard of mosquitoes, squabbling as we went, four of us carrying the erected tent down the road followed by this ancient motorhome and trying to keep track of the dog, since we couldn't find either leash. Then Lisa pointed out that we must look like some demented Memorial Day parade and began to sing "America the Beautiful." All around us, the other campers edged into their tents and RVs and closed the doors behind them.

By then it was pitch dark, of course, so when we finally got the motorhome settled we sent the kids out to the tent to sleep, only to hear horrifying screams when they had a Close Encounter of the Arachnid Kind. Spiders. Luckily there was only one older couple within earshot, and they insisted the next day that they really hadn't heard a thing. Of course, at that point the kids were over there mooching ketchup because I forgot to take any along and who can eat a hamburger without ketchup? I think by then the couple would have said or done anything to humor us. Shortly thereafter, they began to pack up their gear and by dawn's early light, they were gone.

Meanwhile, the kids had gone up the hill to take showers. Since supper was about ready and they had promised to be quick about it I was surprised when they didn't return for a long time. Ray and I, no fools, ate while

91

the food was hot. Eventually Mollie limped back into camp wearing only one sneaker and reporting that the other had somehow arched high into the room near the ceiling, then fallen into an open space between two shower stalls.

The next day, with bungee cord and rope, Ray retrieved the sneaker and earned his fishing badge. Meanwhile, the girls and I went to the pool, where they bravely dodged preparations with Sun Protection factors ranging from 8 to 30 and in the process acquired the first major sunburn of the season.

It's still 24 hours before the real first day of summer, and already I have titled the season: The summer of Sun and Spiders. And I also remember now why we put up with all this—because it's infinitely better than staying home.

They also acquired over the weekend an extra towel, a nice Yale sweatshirt, an unfamiliar cotton shirt, a pair of white canvas shoes, and a pile of teen magazines.

2005 update: Instead of a motorhome we now have a little travel trailer, purchased specifically because it's just big enough for two people, and neither of them is our offspring.

1994

Our Closets Are Stuffed...With Stuff

Everybody knows how it's supposed to be with hangers. You bring home clothes from the store on hangers, you pick up stuff from the cleaners on hangers, Great Aunt Tilly gives you a set of crocheted hangers every birthday, the kids decorate hangers at Scouts or camp — and of course, in the depths of your dark closets those hangers get up to hanky panky and before you know it, you have tangled hangers everywhere you look and it's off to the recycling center with them.

Not around here. For some reason, there never seem to be enough hangers. Where hangers multiply in other people's houses, instead, clothes multiply at the Brackens'. Not "something to wear," you understand (because neither of my adolescent daughters has "a thing to wear"), but stuff that is stained, outdated, torn, unraveling, uglier than dirt, or just plain outgrown.

The end result is closet space that is filled with stuff nobody would be caught dead in, and no hangers for the things we actually don from day to day. The simple solution, I'm told, is to clean out the closets and get rid of the deadwool (and deadpolyester), so to speak.

But I have news for you: It's even easier to keep the closet doors shut and ignore it — as long as you remember to duck when you open them.

Naturally, the end result is a lack of closet space. I sometimes remember fondly all the cupboard space I had in my first apartment — with nothing to put in it. Now, with several sets of cookware, dishes to use daily, Great-Grandma's dishes for holidays, a set of dishes for cooking and serving Chinese specialties (sort of like separate dishes for kosher, now that I think if it), dozens of coffee mugs for every occasion, and a gourmet shop's worth of gadgets, our only solution has been to add closet and cupboard space.

And we have. We added closets upstairs in 1988, closets downstairs in 1989, and kitchen closets in 1992. Funny thing. They're all full now, even the pantry.

How did we allow this to happen? Let me cite one small example that will illuminate the problem. Ray comes home from the supermarket with, among other things, a can of sauerkraut.

Me: "Why'd you buy sauerkraut?"

He: "It was on sale."

Me: "Everybody hates sauerkraut."

He: (as if it explains everything) "But it's *German-style* sauerkraut?"

Me: "By definition, isn't all sauerkraut *German-style?*"

There being no reasonable response to this searing logic, he attempts none. He puts the can in the pantry and it's still there, along with a lot of other stuff we'll probably eat. Someday.

In the meantime, finding a can of tuna fish (if there's any left, which I doubt) is a half-hour proposition, and before it turns up, we've opted for peanut butter, which happens to be right in the front.

We had a linen closet built into the downstairs hall. It seemed like a good idea at the time — keep towels, paper goods, and spare linens near the extra bath and the guest rooms (read: "sleep sofas"). Handy.

That was a great idea, too. Except it hasn't worked. The top shelf of the closet is filled with Ray's much-maligned bottle collection (well, part of the collection, anyway), the bottom shelf has tools and other stuff left from unfinished painting and wallpapering jobs. The rest of the closet is crammed (that's the only word for it) with puzzles and games.

We shouldn't have needed this linen closet at all, I thought, after we added the upstairs linen closet in 1988, but that one's full, mostly of shampoo bottles. (Lisa's bottle collection, only hers are all partially filled.)

I had a broom closet put in the kitchen in 1992, which was a swell idea, except that (I'm embarrassed to admit this) it isn't tall enough for a broom or a mop. There's not much you can do, I've discovered, with a 36" space.

When we gave up the attic (such as it was) in favor of more living space, two things happened. I designated half of the under-the-eaves closet space as "family attic" and the other half as personal closets. Ray and I got half of that personal half, and Lisa the rest. Ours is fine — perfectly adequate, as long as we keep the doors shut and the cats out. For some reason, it reminds them of a sandbox.

Lisa's, on the other hand, is indescribable. I'm not sure I can blame her for the dearth of hangers, because she apparently has no clue what to do with them. I can't say for sure, because nobody's been able to get near the closet for some time now — including the half that I optimistically call the "attic," the place where we stash Christmas ornaments and cat carriers.

One other thing happened when we de-commissioned the original attic. All the junk that was in it was moved to the garage. Remember what I said about Fibber McGee and Mollie's closet? Same thing happens when we open the garage door. Haven't had a car in there since 1988, with no relief in sight.

It's spring again, season for major house over-hauling for those so inclined. (You know who you are.) Not me. But I realize I'll have to do something soon. A couple of options occur to me. I could barricade Lisa in her room until she straightens things out — removing the phone so she can't rat on me to the social welfare people.

I could have a giant yard sale and get rid of the good stuff in the garage, then have a contractor turn the place into a giant closet, maybe one of those European-style upscale things with bins and crates. Or I can ignore the whole thing for another year.

I chose the latter option, with one improvement. I brought home from work a whole bunch of unused hangers in the probably vain hope that the kids would actually use them instead of throwing stuff on the floor of the closet and quickly shutting the door. Out of sight, out of (Mom's) mind.

But there's one up side to all this. There ain't no skeletons in the Bracken closets.

No room for them.

Jeanne Bracken now understands the origin of all those kids' closet terrors. Frankly, some of the stuff in her closets terrifies her, too

2005 update: We remodeled the kitchen with a lot of new cabinets and a real broom closet. They're all full. As for the garage, let's just say a whole new generation of stuff has found a home there.

1995

Summer the Whining Season

School has been out for maybe three weeks now, as I write this on a beautiful summer morning – not too hot, not too humid, too bad I have to go to work...Or maybe not. Summer is of course The Whining Season. ("There's nothing to do. Take us to Hampton Beach. Play a game with us. It's hot. We're out of soda...bread...milk... Take us to an amusement park. I want to go to Jamaica... the Virgin Islands... Maine...")

Heading off for work doesn't get parents off the hook, either, unless they have a job without a telephone at the ready. Those jobs, however, in my experience involve stuff like roofing tar and shovels that I would personally rather not deal with, especially in the Dog Days of Summer. I'd rather be inside the library than on the roof.

Which is not to say I've been totally shirking my Mother Duty. No way. For instance, one day I came home and found five kids in the living room---two of them mine, one a neighbor, one a best friend and one I didn't recognize. When a knock on the door announced a lady I'd never seen before, I foolishly assumed she'd come for the Unknown Teen.

Wrong. She'd come, it transpired, to pick up one of my kids. Even though the explanation was obvious and she was a new babysitting client, it was clear to me that things had gotten a little out of hand.

So I called all the kids onto the porch, away from the lure of television and videos, and laid down the rules for the summer. Parents everywhere are invited to enlarge them and hang them on the refrigerator, possibly with an artfully drawn frame.

1. If you dirty it, wash it. (This includes clothes, dishes and pets.) Towels do not leap, sodden, from

piles in the corner into the washing machine. Left in the heap, beach clothing will develop a life of its own and infest everything within breathing space. There are at least two hampers in the house, not to mention a handy-dandy washer/dryer combination in the cellar, a supply of soap/bleach/fabric softener, hot and cold running water, and a constant supply of electricity to the washer and natural gas to the dryer. Make friends with it.
2. If you take it out, put it back.
3. If you spill it, clean it up.
4. If you use it up, put it on the shopping list.

I'm sure you can think of things to add to the list, but that should get the conversation rolling. I am not complaining about all these kids around the house. They're nice kids and don't give me any more trouble collectively than my own two hand out---in fact, there is a slim possibility that a 13 year-old will be marginally less rude to a parent when a friend is around to watch. But not much.

Anyway, we stocked up on bologna, tuna, peanut butter, and bread, and I went back to work confident, after my jury-related absence, of a warm welcome that had nothing to do with the level of the air-conditioning. With all that rule-setting, I still forgot the Cardinal Caveat of Childrearing: Do Not Be Vague. And its Adjunct Adage: Do Not Assume Your Spouse Is Living on the Same Planet You Inhabit.

On my second day back at work, Lisa called.

"Mom, I've been thinking about this for a long time..."

"If that's the case, can't it wait until dinner?" I asked.

"I want to get it today..."

"Get what?" I wondered, shoes? Clothing for college? A life?

"See, Skeeter is lonely and I'd like to get him another male rabbit for company."

I snorted to myself. Just two days before, Ray had been ranting about the rabbit, the rabbit's unfortunate habit of chewing on the dining room rug, the kids' unfortunate reluctance to clean up after the rabbit... In short, I knew there was no way we were going to get another rabbit. I also saw an opportunity to make Someone Else the final arbiter (read: bad guy).

"I'm not the one you have to convince," I said.

"Does that mean it's all right with you?"

"You have to ask your father," I said.

"But is it all right with you?"

"If you can get your father to agree," I said, chuckling to myself. I mean, I have been married to this man for 25 years and I know he's a toughie. I went back to sorting a week's worth of mail.

Two hours later the phone rang. "Mom! You have to see the bunny. It's so cute! Dad liked the gray one..."

When I could get a word in edgewise, I fairly shrieked, "What! He agreed?" I confronted him that night when I got home --- the rug, I said, the cage, the scattered herbs.

"But they said it was all right with you!" he defended himself.

Aside from the basic feeling that I'd been "had," a victim of the oldest ask-your-other-parent ploy in the world, dating back at least to Cain and Abel, I soon discovered that there was another slight problem with the bunny.

We already had Skeeter Rabbit, right? And now we have Binnie Bunny, okay? Well, guess what! I am assured that it is virtually impossible to tell males from females, and we now are the proud possessors of one of each.

If you think it's hard keeping hormone-charged teens apart, try rabbits.

Whole Lotta Meltin' Goin' On

As I write this, the official start of spring is several days in the future, although the temperature has moderated to the point that the piles of snow are slowly turning into puddles of slush dammed in place by deep ruts of ice.

Ah, March! No offense to any of you Pisces out there, but this is probably my least favorite month of the year—even worse than April's Tax Hell Season (which has the mitigating circumstance that my birthday falls smack in the middle and I usually at least get a good restaurant meal out of it.)

I wouldn't bet, though, that winter is over for us, and I have good reasons for making this prediction. You remember Typhoid Mary, who was not ill with the disease but who was a carrier? Well, I'm Winter Jeanne. I'm a carrier. Trust me, where I am, there will be winter.

Case in point. We had some cold weather in January and some snow off and on earlier in the season. For a couple of weeks in mid-February, though, things were pretty quiet here, weather-wise.

That's because I was in Anchorage. That Alaskan city had been having a very mild winter with very little snow. They were worried because their big winter carnival features sprint sled-dog races, and the ground was almost bare. This is not a problem in the city itself, because snow can be trucked in to cover the streets, but in the back country, that is obviously impossible. A decision had to be made so that the mushers could make or change their plans.

There was great disappointment in The Last Frontier when the races were cancelled. Against my advice, I might add. I had e-mailed my reassurances to people in Anchorage that the Brackens would be arriving several days before the scheduled races and that would solve the no-snow problem. Apparently they didn't believe me.

Yep, I was right. We flew into Anchorage at 11 pm on Saturday. By midnight it was snowing, and the white stuff fell for two whole days. Alaskans, being an intrepid type, were happy to see the storm, although there were some complaints because the buses were running 5 or 10 minutes behind schedule. I never did see a snowplow there.

After a few days of spinning tires and flying slush, the snow more or less took care of itself. The city got about 18 inches of snow and the outlying areas up to 30 inches, but no schools were cancelled. I spent a day at a high school talking to students about writing, and I had to negotiate more than a foot of snow in the unplowed parking lots.

Having delivered snow to Alaska, Ray and I came home to Littleton where the weather had been relatively benign during our absence. But not for long: Within a few days of our return, we had a snowstorm that dumped several inches of the stuff in our driveway. With the help of our faithful plow contractor, we dealt with it.

Less than a week later, though, the weather people went into high gear, with pre-empted programming to warn of A Dreadful Storm heading our way. Storm of the century. Twin to the 1978 Blizzard. A Bad One, Folks!

Panic set in. Store shelves were cleared of life's basics, like toilet paper, and snow shovels sold out in the hardware stores. The Day dawned, with the Brackens headed into Boston for a minor medical procedure that we were assured absolutely, positively could not wait for a few more days. With most people staying at home, we actually made good time into the city. (The doctor, on the other hand, was two hours late.) We were relieved to reach home safely, especially after a couple of hours in the hospital waiting room watching ever-escalating televised dire predictions about The Storm.

While the forecasters had really gone overboard, I did enjoy two snow days in a row, a rarity in my working world. (But those school cancellations running at the bottom of the TV screen during "Jeopardy" really messed up the show.)

On the other hand, I am not eager to see any more snow fall this season, because we are suffering from Short Driveway Syndrome: so little plowed space, so many cars. We can squeeze all of the cars in, but then we are too tightly parked to open the doors to get out.

There being a winter overnight street parking ban, Ray is playing a daily game of Chicken with the police, who have ticketed him twice so far.

Actually I suspect that at least the first ticket was a result of mouthing off at the officer. Ray is not at his finest at 5 am standing deep in snow and waving a shovel. But then, who is?

Spring must be on the way, though. The calendar says so, and besides, Lisa saw robins yesterday and the Red Sox are already squabbling in Florida.

With Opening Day approaching, can May be far behind?

Jeanne Bracken isn't really complaining, because the storms held off until she had flown through three airports, and besides, she got out of Seattle before the earthquake.

In the holy estate of matrimony

1991

Tooling Around the House

My friend Linda just bought her first house and allows as how she had no idea what she was getting into. We all know perfectly well that in buying a house, the real estate people and the bankers all factor income, interest, down payment, points, tax breaks, and utilities into the deal. What they never mention (and if they did, they'd never close a deal) is the new homeowner's first trip to Ye Olde Hardware Store. They never tell you about tools.

When Linda was telling me about that sobering event, I just shook my head in sympathy. I didn't have the heart to tell her what she's up against. But you and I know perfectly well that no former apartment dweller, however well-equipped, can possibly be ready for home ownership without tool purchases whose ultimate cost will rival the annual budget of Albania.

And that's how it should be. You may not have noticed this, but there are fewer gas stations around these days. Instead we now have a hardware store or a lumber yard on every street corner. If we want to get the area economy moving, what we need to do is sell half a dozen Lindas their first houses, then sit back while they go buy tools. We'll be in Fat City by Christmas. Easy.

You think I'm kidding about this? No way. Remember all those organized types you know who have the cellar workshop walls and the garage paneled with fiberboard covered with hooks from which hang a gazillion tools, each with its outline painted carefully in red paint? Each pipe wrench, each hacksaw has its place and its use. There are little drawer things with screws, nuts and bolts, all sorted nearly according to size and function.

This does not come cheaply or easily. Invariably, these painted-tool-outline types are coupled with leave-it-where-it-falls people, and the strain on marriage counselors alone is appalling. It's even worse if they have kids, and let's face it, most of them do. Kids don't leave tools where they fall; they stick them in the clothes dryer or under a bike helmet on the porch.

Anyway, as anyone knows who's been to a hardware store lately, there is a tool for every purpose. Around here, we have hammers: ball peen hammers, sledge hammers, tack hammers, claw hammers. You want to measure something? There is a 10-foot tape measure and a 12-foot tape measure and as of two weeks ago, courtesy of a carpet shop, there are a couple of yardsticks. (The old ones broke somewhere along the line, so when we were invited to take one, we doubled it.)

We also have a T-square that belongs to my brother, but he'll probably need that back now, since he just bought a house. Dad had a folding ruler, too, but apparently Ray hasn't yet realized he doesn't have one. When he does, you can be sure he'll need one.

We have a table saw, a bunch of different hand saws, a portable electric saw, a chain saw. (Ray doesn't know about Dad's jig, band, and reciprocating saws, either.) I have no idea how many screwdrivers there are around the place, but I do know that I have a set of little ones right here in my computer desk drawer. Not because I'm likely to use them on the computer, certainly; the mere idea strikes terror in my low-tech heart. No, I keep them here because nobody else knows I have them, and I intend to keep it that way.

Putty knives? We have 3-inch firm and 3-inch flexible, 1-inch all-purpose. You name it, we've got one. They're all covered with ancient goop and wouldn't smooth putty on a bet.

There are pliers and wrenches and a lot more stuff, but you get the idea. Needle-nose pliers have two primary uses round the house: adjusting the sound on the TV set and turning off the desk lamp with the switch that only works in the "on" mode.

Gardeners have a whole different category of tools. We've got forks, shovels (long-handled, short-handled), rakes (garden, leaf). Hand garden tools are an industry in themselves. They are really good items for economic recovery, because they are something you have to replace every year: wide trowels, narrow trowels, bulb diggers, cute little rakes that cause major pain when you step on them in the dark barefoot, dandelion diggers.

These don't wear out in a year; it's just that sometime between October and those first nice days in March, they self-destruct. Especially if you have kids and you're silly enough to build them a sandbox.

I have something else to say to Linda and all you other new homeowners out there in Hardware Heaven. The most important thing to know about tools has nothing to do with picking the right one for the job.

It's this, Linda: whatever the tool might be, when the time comes to use it, you won't be able to find it.

2005 update: Jeanne begged people not to tip her family off about the secret screwdriver set. It disappeared and she replaced it. Now let's keep this one quiet, okay?

1992

Summertime's Thrill with the Grill

I have been saying for years that Ray is the only man east of the Mississippi born without the crucial barbecuing gene.

All summer long, while my friends sit on their porches with tall cool drinks watching their husbands cook dinner on their gas grills, I have slaved over a hot stove in the kitchen. When I spotted an apron with military decorations emblazoned "Grill Sergeant," I had to buy it — for my brother-in-law, who is a major outdoor chef. Not Ray.

Or so I thought. Oh, he was not entirely without grill experience. We bought a little gas grill to use when camping and he'd gamely sizzle away with hot dogs or whatever. The trouble was, the fire kept going out. I knew that was a hazard with charcoal, but this was the first time I'd experienced snuffout with a gas grill. After all, my friends' husbands seemed to do fine. What he needed, I thought, was experience.

As it turned out, what he really needed was less tin foil. With his fear of fat fires, he'd covered the whole thing with tin foil and expected the fire to somehow burn sans oxygen. Doesn't work. After taking about two hours to grill some pork chops, we figured it out.

That was a couple of years ago and I decided this spring to go for it. I announced that his Father's Day gift would be a nice gas grill for the backyard. He allowed as how that would be nice.

So we headed off for a major department store that was advertising a grill sale, picked out one that didn't have a whole lot of bells and whistles, side burners, whatever, and picked it up. I say "picked it up" advisedly, because this sucker weighs a ton and actually "picking it up" was courting a hernia. We got it in the car, got it home and out to the porch.

There it sat, in its box, for several days while we steeled ourselves for what we knew would be a major marriage challenge. We had heard all the stories about putting these babies together. The mother and son team who took so long to get it assembled that they ate their first grilled meat at 11 p.m. The team of two girls who took five hours.

Ray started in on it one Saturday while I was at work. When I got home, he said "something was wrong." The problem is, the grill may be made in the USA, but the directions were surely printed in Korea by someone for whom English was an unknown language. Besides which, the illustrations (which Ray persists in calling "cartoons") left a lot to be desired.

There is a careful list of parts, including "grease cup ass'y," "external tooth lockwasher #10," "external tooth lockwasher 3/8," "washer burner retention," "#10-24 Square Nu" (sic) and "#10-24 x 1-1/2 Truss RHSMS" (the latter not pictured. I still don't know what it is.) But there is absolutely no picture of the assembled grill.

There were even pictures on the box of the tools needed to complete the job (screwdrivers, wrench, pliers) but nothing to illustrate what success would look like.

Off we headed to the major department store to take a look at the floor model. We thought we figured out what was wrong, bought a barbecue mitt and tongs and left. Cogitating about it over a soft drink, we wavered. Went back to the major department store, looked again, bought a wire basket and a grill cover and listened to the salesman laugh about the calls he gets from livid customers certain that parts are missing from their grill "kits."

"You're really going whole hog," he noted.

"Um...will you be here tomorrow if we call?" we asked.

"Nope!" he said cheerfully. We were not encouraged by his glee.

But the next day we tackled the project anew, partially disassembled what Ray had so laboriously accomplished, put it back together the right way, finished the job, then organized the grill mitt, tongs and wire basket on the porch.

Despite large warnings printed on all the boxes, assembly instructions and use and care manual, the grill is still on the porch (with its combustible ceiling — a clear and present danger.) I'm not too worried about it, though, because we have yet to get the gas tank filled. Ergo, we also have yet to test the gas for leaks ("Do Not Smoke While Testing Gas") and we certainly have yet to enjoy our first morsels of grilled/seared/charred meat.

But when that day comes, I know exactly what I'm going to say to Ray. As I settle down on the porch with a tall cool one, I'll smile sweetly at Ray, standing out on the lawn batting mosquitoes, and say, "Happy Father's Day, Dear, now *you* can cook."

2005 update: We never did get the gas hooked up to that grill. A while later we bought an electric one and donated the gas grill to the church yard sale, where somebody got a great bargain—fully assembled.

Food Fight

The man cannot be trusted in a grocery store. For the past few years, Ray has been in charge of the weekly shopping. I use the term "in charge" advisedly, because it's one place he can't exercise his plastic, but frankly, for a guy who has worked in supermarkets at various times in his life he is remarkably naïve.

For one thing, he doesn't read labels. This is probably not a hanging offense, but in this "healthy" era, it's at least a misdemeanor. For another, shopping should be pretty simple, since he uses a food service that delivers meat, fish, poultry, some prepared and canned foods, paper goods and frozen vegetables right here to the house twice a year. Big orders of meat, fish, etc., etc. So the weekly trip to the market should be a piece of cake, right?

HAH! The system around the house is basic. When someone uses up most or all of something, they write it on the list. Hanging right there on the side of the refrigerator, in red marker. (Well, it should be a red marker, which erases, but too often it's some other color, which doesn't. So the lists from week to week tend to bleed a little.)

At least that's how it's supposed to work. Of course it doesn't. Which is why on Thursday mornings, about 6 a.m., Ray and I sit down to make up the shopping list. He remembers we're almost out of dishwasher detergent; one point for him. We need eggs. I add rye bread to the list; left to his own devices, he'd live on that pasty white stuff and hamburger rolls. We're low on ketchup and the girls have written almond extract, spicy brown mustard and fresh strawberries on the list. Fresh strawberries are not in season. I tell him to skip that and get whatever fruit is on sale.

After work he heads for the store and comes home with his prizes. None of the fruit looked good, he said, so he bought potato chips instead. He remembered the rye bread (and a package of hamburger rolls), ketchup, cat litter, cat food, a six-pack of canned chili, half a dozen cans of flavored tomatoes (I like them plain), two pounds of sausage and a 38-oz. can of green beans. No eggs, but Halloween is only a month away, so he's bought a generous supply of candy for visiting goblins. Dream on!

The next week the kids want almond extract, spicy brown mustard, and turkey for sandwiches. I forget to tell him about the rye bread, so he brings home the pasty white stuff and hamburger rolls, some sugary cereal ("It was on sale."), a cake mix and a can of frosting ("There was a coupon."), two more pounds of sausage, turkey bologna (which the kids hate), more potato chips, a head of lettuce and a supply of Halloween candy to replace what's been eaten. (All of it.)

Week three the budget is tight, so we agree that we don't need much. He staggers home with half a dozen bags laden with all-beef-bologna, corn flakes (the kids finished off the sugary cereal in about one day), four cans of spaghetti sauce (to keep the 11 already in the cupboard company, I presume), some more flavored tomatoes, four boxes of Hamburger Helper, the makings of two pumpkin pies, and three dozen eggs. Plus more Halloween candy.

The cupboard is stuffed with canned chili, spaghetti sauce, flavored tomatoes, boxes of cereal the kids won't eat, a 25-lb. bag of rice he found on a markdown shelf, four jars of yellow mustard, six bottles of dishwashing liquid, cans of green beans and jars of jellies of every flavor and description (including cranberry!). We sit down on Thursday morning, Week Four, at the crack of dawn and go over the list. I tell him we don't need chili, spaghetti sauce, flavored tomatoes, cereal, rice, yellow mustard, dishwashing liquid, green beans, or jelly. We do need spicy brown mustard and almond extract, milk, bread (I specify rye), salad makings, and vinegar.

He comes home with Pop Tarts, pancake mix, syrup (that makes four bottles in the pantry), chips, turkey salami, honey wheat bread (he loves anything with the name "honey" in it, probably because nobody else does and he gets it for himself), more cat food, another bottle of yellow mustard, and vanilla extract. He has found cantaloupes, bananas, apples, and potatoes to his liking. Also another supply of Halloween candy. He has also gotten some instant hot cereal, which the kids like, but in honey nut flavor, which they don't.

The next week I go through the pantry and give Ray a long list of things we don't need, like fruit, since last week's supply is beginning to draw flies. Obviously, this is an exercise in futility, since he can come up with dozens of coupon and sale items that I would never dream of telling him we don't need.

The kids want spicy brown mustard and almond extract, and I'd like low fat cheese. He comes home with potatoes, eggs, another pound of sausage (to join the two in the freezer), two pounds of bacon (four in the freezer already), cat food, honey rolls, more bananas, more apples ("But they're golden, and we only had red!"), Mootown Snackers, dried fruit rolls, regular cheese ("No, they didn't have any lowfat cheese."), cottage cheese (with pineapple, which I loathe), hamburger rolls, and another few cans of spaghetti sauce. Also more Halloween candy.

This has been going on for years now, and I doubt it will change in this lifetime. Since I'm not willing to give up a couple of hours a week, even to save $40, there probably is no viable solution except to grin and bear it – and eat a lot of canned spaghetti sauce and green beans.

But there is good news and bad news. The good news is, Halloween is over for another year and by the time the goblins got here, there was still some candy corn left (nobody really likes it here).

The bad news is, we still need spicy brown mustard and almond extract.

Men and Women Are Worlds (and Malls) Apart

By now pretty much everybody has at least heard about the major, best-selling book *Men are from Mars, Women are from Venus.* There are the hard- and soft-cover editions, not to mention the recorded versions and heaven knows what else. (Mars dolls? Venus stickers? The mind boggles.) Heck, probably a whole bunch of people have actually read the book, given all those copies floating around.

Not me. I haven't bought any copies at all. Not hard-cover, not soft-cover, not even tape. The occasional visitor to my home office might disagree, pointing to a *MafMWafV* tape set (abridged, I believe) on a top shelf out of the reach of the cats. I'm not being picky semantically here. The fact is, I was given the tapes by an editor who was barely able to contain her amused disdain with the book. She and her teen-age daughter listened to the book and said it was "absurd"--her term.

With that dubious recommendation in mind, and considering my motto, "So many books, so little time," I somehow have not made it a priority to fit *MafMWafV* into my life.

I have only once mildly regretted not reading *MafMWafV*, and that was sometime last week when I saw a newspaper article advocating practical gifts for Valentine's Day. The piece was called "Women are from Venus, Men are from Sears," as I recall.

Catchy. Lousy advice, though. I wasted no time getting the paper out of sight before Mister Truck Driver could get any funny ideas, but there was little doubt in my mind that behind that clever title lurked evil in the heart of the writer. It must have been a male journalist, because no sister worthy of girlfriend status would have given such radical, mutinous, revolutionary, destructive, dumb advice.

So, even though Valentine's Day is behind us for another year, let me explain this one more time, before some poor guy messes up on an anniversary, birthday, or Christmas.

Here is the truth: Men are from Aubuchon's; women are from Tiffany's. He's off pricing vacuum cleaners and she's window shopping for tennis bracelets. Or--and this actually happened in our family a few years ago--she wants Schwinn, he buys Tupperware. It was a lot of Tupperware, admittedly, but even sheer volume didn't overcome that goof.

Actually, there was a valuable lesson in that exchange: Ladies, do not assume that he will read your mind, pick up on your hints or conspire with your best friends to select just the perfect token of his love and admiration. After the Tupperware fiasco (heck, it was even stored in the garage, under a blanket I was forbidden to approach, just like-- well--a bicycle), I learned to clip pictures of gifts I would welcome, mark the colors and sizes as appropriate, and post them on the refrigerator at least a month ahead of time.

Because believe me, men cannot be trusted alone in stores, specialty or otherwise. And if some subversive journalist is out there telling them we want practical gifts, well, you can just imagine the results. Practical, he thinks. Electric broom, mountain tent, car wax kit, set of tires (well, they have diamond-patterned treads some of the time, and he'd pay to have the guys at the shop install and balance 'em, so what's the beef?).

While he's thinking those thoughts, she's defining practical in her own way. Jacuzzi, diamond earrings, a watch without a major cartoon character on the face, a weekend in London, a Caribbean cruise, a lock on the bathroom door so she can take an hour-long bubble bath without interruptions by the phone, offspring or pets, or, if he really wants to talk practical, she'd settle for weekly

Maid service.

He thinks a great evening is takeout from the sub shop, eaten in front of the TV during a John Wayne video marathon. She's thinking of ballroom dance lessons for two, with an elegant evening on the town to practice.

His idea of fancy is a little something (a very little something) from Victoria's Secret. She figures OK, as long as she gets to wear it in Cancun, bedroom temperatures anywhere north of the tropics requiring chin-to-toe flannel for survival this time of year.

His idea of luxury is valet parking at the pizza place. Her idea of luxury involves a limo and orchestra seats.

His favorite tickets: the Celtics. Hers: "Riverdance."

His wheels: Corvette. Hers: Caravan.

His magazine: "Discovery Channel." Hers: *Caribbean Life and travel.*

His spectator sport: wrestling. Hers: giant slalom.

His TV star: Ted Koppel. Hers: Oprah.

His libation: Bud. Hers: Guinness.

His dessert: Little Debbie's. Hers: Godiva.

His weekend retreat involves a backpack and the top of Ole Smoky. Hers requires lobster fireside at a coastal Maine inn.

Frankly, it's a wonder the species survives.

No Kitchen Flies On Me

I can't remember ever having such a problem with bugs in the house.

I suppose it is lucky that we are dealing here with bugs of the insect persuasion and not of the computer variety, which can be a lot more devastating. Anyway, it's been years since I had to worry about moths eating sweaters, and all of the various termite inspections required for mortgage refinancing have been negative. Window and door screens keep the mosquito population at bay for most of the summer, and flies have just never been that much trouble.

Until now. I don't know what it is, but for the past couple of months we have been plagued by flies. We aren't doing anything any differently, as far as I know. Sure, we have pets, but we clean up after them as often as we ever did—which is to say, less regularly than I might like but a whole lot more than the family "slaves" (just ask them!) would prefer. For that matter, the flies are not congregating in the rooms where the pets hang out, but mostly in the kitchen.

Okay, we're not going to win any *Better Homes and Gardens* award, but we don't have to duck the Board of Health, either. We remove trash, wash dishes, bag the compost, empty wastebaskets, rinse cans and bottles for recycling, and clean the floor on a fairly regular basis.

So why this visitation of flies? In the winter? Ray thought the culprit might be Lisa's flower-bulb-forcing-adventure, which began about the same time the little buggers appeared. I can't think what that would have to do with it, but I'm no expert.

Whatever the reason, I told Ray we had to do something about it.

He agreed.

I mean, we don't even own a fly swatter; that's how rare it is that we have flies. I have no compunction about killing them with rolled newspapers, folded magazines or whatever other lethal weapon might be handy, although the mesh swatters do seem more efficient, probably for some aerodynamic reason I couldn't possibly explain.

I went to work and Ray went off to the hardware store. When I got home, I discovered that he had gone the low-tech, passive route. Instead of getting a few swatters, he had obtained a bunch of those old-fashioned sticky flypaper rolls. He had hung one in the downstairs bathroom, where it had already snagged a score of varmints. The other dangled from the beam between living room and kitchen, over the microwave, where it was doing its deadly best to rid us of these pests. I figured things were under control.

After a few days, the flypaper was heavily, well, fly-ed, and the air seemed clear. Ray threw it away and we heaved a sigh of relief. Too soon. Maybe the next generation of flies hatched; come to think of it, all of these flies are really, really small—babies, really.

Whatever. We were again overrun—or, more precisely, overflown—with flies. I got another flypaper from the box and tacked it to the overhead beam out of the way near the kitchen door. Before long it was doing its catch-the-flies-and-kill-them thing. Ray figured that once a bunch of flies had been caught the remaining contingent would be unlikely to make the same fatal mistake, but let's face it: flies are pretty dumb.

Still, having a bunch of dead flies hanging overhead leaves a lot to be desired, so again we threw away the used roll. Sure enough, in a day or two they were baaaaaaack.

That night I came home from work and discovered that Ray, the Master of the Fly Universe, had hung the new flypaper roll from the kitchen light fixture, where it dangled into the middle of the room. Right in the path of anyone trying to cook dinner, straighten the kitchen, get a snack or feed the dog. By bedtime we had not only a whole raft of flies stuck to it but also generous samples of Lisa's and my hair. You have not lived until you have pivoted, hot frying pan in hand, and found yourself glued to sticky paper with a bunch of dead bugs.

You would think, since Ray is taller than me or Lisa, that it would pose a similar problem for him, but apparently either a) he has too little hair to get stuck to it, or b) he spends entirely too little time in the kitchen.

We have repeated the scenario several times now: Ray hangs a new flypaper roll in the middle of the kitchen, I hit the ceiling (and also the flypaper) and tear it down, a new family of flies moves in, he hangs another roll from the light fixture, I walk into it... This is a man who stores groceries in such inaccessible places that I need a ladder to reach them, yet for some bizarre, guy reason, he insists on having the flypaper really, really handy—or maybe that should be head-y.

At the moment we're on a down cycle—the fly population is under control, the kitchen airspace is free of glue-y spirals, and it's possible to sweep the floor without losing a bunch of hair.

I suppose before long we'll have another swarm of flies. Still, I'm going to hide the rest of the flypaper rolls and go buy some fly swatters.

And if Ray hangs anything sticky from the kitchen light fixture, I'll use the fly swatter on him.

Domestic abuse. You heard it here first.

I wouldn't have minded so much if the flypaper had snagged only the gray hairs.

2005 Update: Just the other day Ray bought a new bunch of flypaper rolls and hung one where I would walk into it in the bathroom. The same day he had his head shaved. He said he went bald because there was little enough hair there to worry about anyway, but I have my doubts.

To love, comfort and honor

Is Anybody There?

Take it from me—when you write each week in the newspaper about your kids' oddities, you have a tough time finding babysitters. So I was especially pleased the other day when my friend Natalie offered to take Mollie off my hands one morning when I was supposed to work.

"Are you sure? Do you know what you're getting into?" I asked her. "Remember, this is the kid who has been called the 80-year-old-midget."

"Oh, yes," she said, admitting that she was not being entirely altruistic. Her four-year-old son, she added, needs playmates. "I mean," she said, "he sits at the dinner table going on and on about his friend Bobby, Bobby's house, Bobby's family. And my husband looks at me and pantomimes, 'Who's Bobby?' and there isn't any Bobby."

When I dropped Mollie off, I reassured Natalie that there is nothing wrong with having an imaginary friend. She should know about the imaginary friends I've had to deal with.

It's all genetic, really, because I think my Mother had imaginary friends, even as an adult. I remember standing in the kitchen where we lived when I was a kid, washing dishes and watching Mom stand outside, hanging up clothes on the line and carrying on a conversation with the sheets. I wasn't sure, of course, who she was talking to, but she would nod, chat, put her hands on her hips, make all those gestures of ordinary over-the-fence-gossip, and she did it so well that I was usually fooled into thinking some neighbor had slipped around the corner of the building when I wasn't looking and that Mom was really talking to someone. She wasn't.

If I had an imaginary friend, I don't remember it. I honestly think the aberration skipped my generation. But both of my kids have had them, with a vengeance. They choose them from their favorite television shows.

Which is why Lisa had the Incredible Hulk following her around for a long time. It was fine while he was in his mild-mannered David Banner guise, but when he lost his temper, look out. Many was the winter auto trip when we had to roll down the windows and push that green monster out of the car. It wasn't easy.

Lisa had Jessica, too, a much more ordinary imaginary friend, boring, even, compared to the Hulk, but she did provide a breather from the Hulk's excitement.

We eventually outgrew the Hulk and Jessica when Lisa moved on to school. But now we have a whole houseful of Mollie's imaginary friends to contend with. They are all based on Masters of the Universe cartoon shows.

Mollie thinks she is She-Ra, she of the improbable bustline, the improbable waist, the improbable flowing mane. I mean, who combs the tangles our of HER hair? I have never watched these cartoons on television, so I am always surprised at what She-Ra is up to. Mollie goes around the house with a chair rung stuffed in the back of her shirt. She whips it out now and then, waving it in the air with a bloodcurdling yell: "I am She-Ra. Princess of Power. By the Power of Gray Skull."

This is unusual behavior, to say the least, and I wonder sometimes what people think, especially when they see the chair rung in her clothing. Ah well, never apologize, never explain.

If it was just She-Ra I had to deal with, that wouldn't be so bad. But we also have Adam the Prince of Eternia, Adora, and a whole carload of other Universe Masters and assorted royalty.

Mollie carries on by the hour about "Adam my brother," "my mother," "my father," and heaven only knows who else. She does not do this quietly. And they are an odd bunch, a least as Mollie reports their escapades. The other day she told me about "my father," describing behavior that would get "my father" arrested if

121

he were to actually do those things on the streets of Littleton. Since she has also created an arresting character to serve the role of "my mother," I know enough to take it with a grain of salt, but I can't help wondering what she's telling the folks at nursery school.

It's not just people, either. She-Ra, Adam and Adora come with a whole assortment of hangers-on. For example, Adam has pets. Not kitty cats, mind you. Not puppies. Not even My Little Ponies. Adam has pet snakes. Plural. Rattlesnakes. Just what I needed slithering around the house.

When Jessica was around, she never got Lisa in trouble, but boy! is Adam ever a handful! He loses my hairbrush, makes Mollie say swears, and make some awful messes.

Blaming Adam does save wear and tear on the dog.

But a therapist would have a field day.

Life Begins at Forty

By now you know, faithful reader, that I recently passed a milestone — my 40th birthday. And I am happy to be able to report from The Other Side that life does indeed begin at (or at least continue after) 40. Let me tell you how it's been.

Ray, who hasn't got a romantic cell in his body, bless him, took all the hints I had made about wanting a microwave for my birthday. I started in around Christmas and even went to the store to pick out the model I wanted.

A week before my birthday I arrived home to find an enormous microwave that takes up roughly a third of the kitchen. It looked a lot smaller in the store. We could fit the entire family in there. Ah well, I am now delving into the joys of microwave cooking — which means that so far I can boil water and heat leftovers. You have to crawl before you can walk.

And that was it as far as my family was concerned, although Lisa did make herself a sticker to wear to school that said "My mother is 40." It was lost on her fourth grade classmates, of course, but the teachers could appreciate the sentiment. I was prepared for the day with a button: "Tease me about my age and I'll beat you with my cane."

Mother gave me a present. Unwrapped. Said "happy birthday." My younger brother and his family didn't even note the day, which is just as well because I have called him "The Kid" for so long that he's bound to start calling me something one of these days. Like "Old Lady."

My sister came through. Because I marked her 40th a couple of years ago with a small nudge, she said all along my turn was coming. She sent flowers, with a balloon attached. "Over the Hill," the black balloon says. This is especially remarkable because a couple of days ago she was driving a car of uncertain vintage and reliability

East from Portland, Oregon, towing a trailer full of household goods over the Rockies. You can always count on my sister in a pinch.

In many respects my birthday was like any other day. I spent the morning dragging a sick child to the doctor's office, getting a prescription filled, rearranging my work schedule for as long as she remained contagious, and trying to get the kid to swallow a teaspoonful of medicine three times a day. But that's another column.

All in all, not the kind of day to write home about, right? Wrong! Because I am here to testify that life begins at 40 — and very early in the morning at that. If you want to have a great birthday, announce it ahead of time in the newspaper and sit back. I got birthday cards and lots of greeting from my friends. And that wasn't all. I had not one but two birthday parties at work (one of the fringe benefits of having more than one job).

My Birthday Eve was eventful, because there seemed to be a lot of cars driving around the neighborhood slowly, dropping off people, lots of noise and general merriment. "The natives are restless tonight." I said to Ray. Then I went to sleep. Little did I know what the natives were up to.

Around 6:20 the morning of B-day, I heard a car honk as it drove past. Then another, and another. Lots of cars honking.

Must be a dog in the street, I thought. Not ours. And rolled over.

More honking. Slowly awakening, I had wondered if the kids were up to something. I decided that there was something on the front door. One the outside. Something black. A shroud. Balloons decorated the railings on the front steps. "Over the Hill" balloons. "We mourn the passing of your youth" balloons. Still cars were honking. There were signs on the telephone poles and trees.

Hastily dressing, I went out to read them. People driving down our main street were reading them, too. "If

124

You Believe...In Life...After 40...Honk!" they read. It was wonderful.

I found out who did this (I would have suspected my sister, but I knew she was out of town.) The perpetrator asked me to save the shroud, because they have another victim lined up a couple of weeks from now.

All day the honking went on. I wasn't about to take down the signs, but fortunately the neighbors thought it was funny. And that wasn't all. Once, going to investigate a flurry of honking, I found a school bus stopped out front, traffic piling up behind it, everybody honking and the kids learning out the window singing "Happy Birthday!" It was wonderful.

Then a reporter came to interview me, bearing a dozen roses and a cake. A friend from Church brought some daffodils. I had so many flowers, I kept checking to make sure I hadn't died. It was wonderful.

In fact, it was so great that I have decided to turn 40 again next year.

So This is the Empty Nest Syndrome

The first I heard about it was one night when, lying in bed, Lisa announced that she and her sister would be going to my Mother's for a week. "And we're taking the kittens with us."

"Uh," I said, "does Grandma know about this?"

"I'm going to call her," she replied. And did. They arranged the whole thing themselves, with Ray and me providing transportation. On Sunday, after insisting that chores be finished, we headed north. A few hours later, Ray and I came south again. Alone. The girls have spent the last few days learning to make dill pickles, picking various late season berries, and I'm not sure what else. Because I haven't heard a word from them since we dropped them off.

This is good. When they're unhappy, they let me know all about it. Meanwhile, it's been pretty quiet around here, once the phone calls looking for babysitters dried up. I heartily recommend this type of hiatus for burned-out parents. Because you know your kids are away if:

There aren't four baskets of clean laundry on the couch waiting for someone to fold and put them away.

The same seven cans of soda (full) are in the pantry day after day.

There are just as many doughnuts in the kitchen when you get up in the morning as there were when you went to bed.

There aren't three odd socks and a single sneaker on the living room floor.

The toilet paper roll lasts for more than a day—and it's on the holder, not on the floor behind the hopper.

The phone rings about a quarter as much as usual—and it's for you.

You have time to read and think and actually get somewhere without an interruption every 6.8 minutes to negotiate the television schedule or a board game.

The TV remote—it's there! Also, pencils, pens, scissors and paper towels.

There's still milk left, and it's in the 'fridge, not in a glass on the bedroom floor.

Dirty laundry is not piling up like autumn leaves.

The portable phone is in its cradle, not under a couch cushion or behind the television.

The TV is off!

You only have to run the dishwasher every four days although you're eating every meal at home.

You spend time wondering where the cat is rather than the kids.

The cat disappears inside the house and isn't found for 12 hours because nobody flops into the recliner where he's hiding among the springs.

At night when you turn out the bedroom lights, the house is actually dark.

Your own clothes are in the drawer rather than on someone else's back. Except that the purple sneakers seem to have gone to Grandma's with the gang.

There is no hair clog in the shower drain.

The towels are still on the rack in the bathroom rather than moldering on someone's bed.

You haven't heard the word "pizza" for a full 96 hours.

It's safe to put your hand on the shelf in the bathtub without risking a finger amputation from an errant razor.

Nobody is fighting over the passenger front seat in the car.

A loaf of bread actually lasts from one weekly grocery run to the next.

You know the kids took the kittens with them because:

The litter boxes don't have to be changed daily. (Talk about food processors!)

You don't have to watch where you step to avoid little tails and paws.

There aren't grubby cat food dishes in every room of the house. (It's tricky to get all these critters fed without them poaching on each other's goodies.)

So OK, it's quiet around here. I'm actually getting some real work done on various writing projects. But you know what?

I miss them. Even the kittens.

2005 update. Empty nest? What empty nest? I really don't mind, except for the soda, donuts, phone...the whole ball of (melted) wax.

Rats! Hamsters are Running up the Bills

My friend Gloria, whose parents ran a pet shop for years, thinks I'm crazy. She says the only reason for getting any pet smaller than a cat is to teach the kids about life and death. Mostly the latter. But then, she likes snakes, so what does she know?

But she may be right. We had goldfish for quite a while, although I can't really see much virtue in fish as pets. They don't sleep on your feet or feel warm and fuzzy or any of those good things. They just swim around in an increasingly murky tank and periodically they go belly up so you replace them. It's good for the economy.

We did better with the rabbit, although she only was with us for a year or two. (I've lost track, but her legacy lives on in a chewed telephone extension wire that I'll have to move my entire home library to replace.) The dog, of course, was practically Methuselah, going to her just reward after nearly 15 years. So far, so good with the cats.

And then there are the hamsters. I couldn't say for sure about cats, but hamsters seem to have at least five lives, counting the times they've gotten loose (three times in a single evening) and avoided being cat chow. I guess I can understand why the cats don't get along all that well — stepfamilies have their own agendas, after all. But these two hamsters came as a pair and should be used to each other by now.

But no. When they're not hiding food or trying to chew their way to freedom, they're fighting. This is not even mildly amusing, since they tend to do physical damage to each other at regular intervals.

This is not because they are ill housed. No, we now have, by actual count, the collected hamster gear from three families who decided to get out of the hamster business. (One of them was Gloria.) That means we have four plastic cages with innumerable tubes, wheels, balls, and various other unidentifiable gadgets — most of them on the living room floor. This does not count the two fish-tank cages, one of which Mollie won at a raffle.

I suspect the raffle was a bag job, and that all the other mothers refused to let their kids "take a chance." I base this on the fact that all of the hamster gear (worth probably zillions of dollars new) was given to us under a solemn vow that we would *never give it back. Ever.*

The hamsters were gifts, too. And (trust me on this one) I would advise to always look a gift hamster in the mouth. I learned this when my friend Judy told me about the death of her kids' hamsters, which starved to death. It seems that the origin of the expression "long in the tooth," meaning greatly aged, was coined about hamsters, which grow their teeth as they get older until they can no longer eat. Voila! One hamster funeral, coming up.

We probably don't need to worry about this, although our hamsters aren't interested in the pretty fruit-shaped and –colored wood pieces we bought for them; they're keeping their incisors in control trying to gnaw their way out of the cages that separate them from a hostile (read: feline) world.

Lisa hates the chewing noise, and the cats are developing nervous twitches from pressing their noses against the clear plastic tubes.

You can, of course, arrange dental surgery for your hamster ($11 each) but the vet assured us it wasn't necessary. I think she was saving us for bigger and better things. Like antibiotics, emergency visits, and maybe even surgery. (I heard of a vet doing open heart surgery on a hamster, so I have to believe it's possible, but unless the vet starts taking Blue Cross — we do, after all, subscribe to a *family plan* — it ain't gonna happen here.)

Anyway, Gloria might be able to let her kids' pets die, but she doesn't live with Mollie. Mollie *cares.* If we do not do everything in our power to make these hamster not only live, but live well, we will have to bear the consequences, and it won't be a pretty sight. Which is why, after the silly rodents got into a fight and one ended up with an eye infection, Ray dashed off to the vet with the little furball. (Mollie went along, too.)

Okay, I admit the swollen eye wasn't the only symptom. The "rat" was having trouble standing up. She kept falling over, and we'd have moments of high drama when she fell over and lay there on her side with her feet in the air.

The bill, counting emergency visit and two medicines, came to $50.89. For that amount, we could have bought about a dozen new hamsters, as Gloria pointed out when she was able to catch her breath from laughing. I noted that next time we'd be prepared, since the antibiotic is the same Lisa takes regularly and we'll just slip one of the pills in her (not Lisa's) Rat Chow.

I'd like to say the doses with eye ointment and medicine droppers have worked wonders, but I'd be lying. The hamster is till under intensive care. Every now and then she falls over and when we set her back on her feet, she just stands there, wobbling ominously.

I was at work when the hamster emergency visit was authorized and executed, so I'm not responsible for any of this.

But I'll tell you one thing. The only one sicker than the ailing hamster around here is the guy responsible for the $50.89 vet bill. We won't mention any names.

I'll give you a hint, though. There are only two guys around here, and one of them has four feet, long gray fur and meows when hungry. If you still can't figure it out, I'll add that Ray rarely meows.

2005 update. The hamsters are long gone. Don't ask.

She could be your mother or mine

She's somewhere in her 80s, although she has never admitted her exact age to me. She's a well-educated, intelligent editor, now retired. She lives alone in a keep-to-yourself apartment complex in another town. She is stubborn, private, stubborn, independent, and...did I mention stubborn?

She made one big mistake. She aged beyond her driver's license in a town without any public transportation at all, not even a senior van. She has been dependent on the kindness of strangers for most of a year now. Unwilling to change her life-long habits, she insists on shopping the European way: daily, for small quantities of bread, milk, cheese, the tiniest bottle of aspirin, the mini-container of instant coffee.

Feisty, her troubles came to a head when she broke her hip last summer. After a few weeks in various hospital settings, she demanded to go home and was sent with a sheaf of social agency referrals.

The home care agency really tried. They sent health aides and physical therapists. She wouldn't let them in the door. The pharmacy sent prescriptions she wouldn't accept. The town sent Meals on Wheels, but she didn't like them. Volunteers delivered groceries but not the specific brand of cheese or type of bread she preferred. One by one, the various volunteers fell by the wayside, some after getting numerous phone calls in a day-- or in an hour. She tended to forget she had already called, or she called in case her request hadn't gotten through, or she called people out of meetings at work for urgent messages. Yeah, she could be difficult. I myself took a several-week hiatus after she called at 6 one morning.

Still, pretty much everybody agreed that having an 80-year-old lady hitchhiking to the store was not appropriate. Finally the home care agency, concerned about her safety and health, asked for a court evaluation of her competency. Rather than giving her advance notice, the social worker appeared at her door and announced an imminent hearing. She wouldn't go.

Frustrated, the social worker went to court herself. A few hours later a pair of uniformed police officers appeared at the woman's door. She opened it only wide enough for them to slip her a subpoena to appear first thing Monday morning.

She called me. She reported that she didn't want to be incarcerated (her term) and I assured her that incarceration was not on her horizon. I explained about the competency hearing and suggested it would be in her best interest to appear. She called repeated over the weekend, deciding (reasonably, I thought) that she wanted a court-appointed attorney to represent her. I checked with the police department and was assured that if she appeared at the appointed hour and asked for a lawyer, the judge would oblige. I arranged to pick her up and drive her to the hearing so she wouldn't have to ride with the now-much-maligned social worker. (She is generally somewhat genteel but can be cranky and, when cornered, goes into pit bull mode.)

She called at 3 on Monday morning to say she wasn't feeling well and wasn't going to court. I am not at my best awakened from a deep sleep (and I wasn't very popular with my also-aroused family, either) so I didn't argue with her. I went to the courthouse anyway. While I was talking with the social worker in the hallway, a woman came over and introduced herself. She was a lawyer appointed to represent the elderly lady's interest. Happy to hear about it, I was still annoyed that nobody in touch with the elderly lady had known about the appointment. Foreknowledge would have at least salvaged part of my weekend.

When the case was called and the judge saw that the woman had not appeared, he signed a warrant. I guess it was an arrest warrant, although that word was never uttered. A squad car with a uniformed officer was prepared to go for her.

What if she won't open the door? I asked. The officers would break in. Handcuffs were mentioned. The lawyer refused to accompany the police officer for ethical reasons. I offered to go, alone. She was ready when I went to her apartment, although she obviously felt betrayed by the social worker, whom she suspects of having her own agenda. I chatted on the way to court, although she accused me of being garrulous to distract her. Guilty as charged. She conferred with her lawyer and with a doctor, then appeared in court. With some hearing loss, she wasn't able to understand all of what was happening, although her lawyer made a valiant attempt to keep her at home or at least to shorten the evaluation period. She was "sentenced" to 10 days in a specialized hospital setting, where she would be evaluated for competency. After the hearing, a court officer escorted her to an elevator and she was taken to the lower level, a secure area, to await an ambulance for transport. I was not allowed to drive her to the hospital. I was not allowed to wait with her in a conference room.

She was put into the holding cell, alone. There wasn't anything more I could do for her, so I went back to work. As I drove, I thought of the tiny, 80-something, white-haired woman, dressed in a tweed coat, skirt and jacket, neck scarf, and crocheted hat.

I forgot the three-calls-in-half-an-hour hassles. I forgot the 6 a.m. phone call, the 3 a.m. phone call. I forgot the "quick errands" that stretched to half a day running around town, several times a week.

I just couldn't shake the image of her sitting in a cell. She was right. She was incarcerated, and her only crime was getting old.

2005 update: The lawyer pointed out that the woman trusted strangers on the highway more than the social service agencies. Her instincts were right on. She never went back to her apartment. After spending weeks in various (locked) hospital wards, she was placed in a series of assisted care facilities by a court-appointed guardian. Her regular calls begging me to take her home eventually tapered off to none.

In sickness and in health

1986

A Pox on Both Your Houses

I knew the chicken pox was around and had reached as close as the next town. I knew this because our friends Pete and Charlene have a teenaged son who came down with them. (Let's call him Mike.) Charlene figured, *Here we go*, expecting all three kids to get them.

Son number one (let's call him Joe) had other plans: No Way! He pitched a tent in the back yard for the duration. But daughter Sissy was sure to get them.

After about two weeks, the daily watch began. Every morning Charlene checked Sissy for telltale spots. Nothing.

Saturday morning, Sissy called to report that she didn't have the pox yet. Since nobody else was up, she told me all about it. Then I went off to work, mentally grateful that my kids hadn't been to Pete and Charlene's for a few weeks and hadn't been with Sissy.

I got home from work late that afternoon to find Sissy playing with my kids. Oh jeez, I said to Ray, Lisa will probably come down with the pox the day she's supposed to leave for camp.

He professed innocence of any chicken pox watch.

The next morning at Sunday school, Lisa started to feel lousy. We whipped her home, discovered she had a temperature of 102, and sent her to bed. Within an hour, she felt fine and wanted to carry on with afternoon plans. No way, I said. That evening she had a fever again, so I kept her home despite her assurances that she felt fine. All day long she cavorted around the house and generally acted perfectly healthy. Meanwhile, I had a couple of conversations with Charlene, who reported that Sissy didn't have the chicken pox yet.

You know, I said to Charlene, Lisa has a couple of spots of something that looks like poison ivy on her forehead. What do these pox look like? She described them, and I said, Nope, that's not what these look like at all.

Tuesday morning I checked Lisa over. She still had poison ivy in a couple of places and a bug bite or two on her back; it is, after all, mosquito season. I sent her to school.

At 9, Charlene called. Sissy was home with a headache and low grade fever, and how was Lisa? I explained that I'd sent her off to school.

Around 9:30, the school nurse called. I think, she said, these really are chicken pox.

Send her home, I said.

When Lisa got here, I was amazed to note that she was by then covered with little bumps with tiny watery blisters in the middle. Exactly like Charlene described.

I called Charlene back. I was supposed to go to Boston, and would she watch Lisa? We both knew that the hazard in the proposal was that, if Sissy didn't already have the chicken pox, she would be exposed to them again. Charlene figured what the heck. Might as well get them over with. Charlene's mother assured her she had had chicken pox as a child, so at least that wasn't a worry.

We conspired not to tell Joe until it was too late for him to move back into the tent, still pitched in the yard. And I went off to Boston to take part in a radio telethon, where I announced that Lisa had not been able to go with me because of chicken pox.

By the time I got home, Sissy was covered with poxes, too. Worse. Charlene reported that Joe had arrived home just as I announced to Greater Boston that Lisa had chicken pox. (How was I to know that a teenager would be listening to Talk Radio?)

Joe, Charlene said, had groaned, OH NO, she just played with Sissy.

Within two days, I knew several things about chicken pox. The itching is combated in two ways. First, you buy either a liquid or a capsule of an antihistamine recommended by our doctor. I'd advise getting the liquid, because the capsules come sealed in virtually indestructible plastic bubble packs that cannot be pierced, sawed, or broken by normal human beings. (When you finally read the directions, you will note that you are supposed to peel off the backing — a simple proposition, perhaps, for a person with fingernails and nerves of steel, but not for *moi*.)

Second, the child should take a bath in baking soda. Run right out and purchase an industrial-size drum of it, because you will need it.

Third, a large bottle of gin will come in handy. (Hint: this is not for the patient.)

That's what I learned about the chicken pox — so far. I also know the incubation period for chicken pox. I figured by the time you read this, Mollie will be covered with little bumps that look like a cross between poison ivy and mosquito bites. I expect that she will come down with them late Wednesday, because I'm supposed to go back to Boston Thursday.

I also learned that there is no prayer of forgiveness in the liturgy for the family that exposes the entire Sunday school to chicken pox.

Charlene learned something else about chicken pox. Your mother might be mistaken about your having had the disease as a child. Your mother might say, as you break out with little poison ivy-mosquito-like bites, "Maybe that was the *measles* you had..."

Anticipating the Terrible Teens

It used to be (well, to be honest, still is) that I would commiserate with my pregnant friends. With a nod of my slightly grayed head at their swollen bellies, I would heave a theatrical sigh and grimace, "Better you than me, honey!"

Then after the bundle of joy had arrived, I would dandle the little dear on my knee or snuggle him or her on my shoulder, remembering—briefly—the lovely feeling I got from those tentative first smiles from my babies. Then the borrowed sweetie would either deafen me with yowling, yank a handful of my hair out by the roots, wrestle my glasses to the floor, or (most often) spit up on me. Another theatrical sigh from me, and the tyke would go back to Mommie. "Better you than me, honey," I'd say with a laugh, mopping at my shoulder.

But now I'm looking at things from another angle. Where until very recently I was able to smugly offer all kinds of advice to new parents—advice from the depths of my parenting experience, all 9½ years of it—I am, some would say, about to reach my level of parental incompetence.

I am nothing if not optimistic, but lately I have been hearing a new four-letter-word from my friends, whose parenting experience often supersedes mine by about five or six years. The new word (dare I use it in polite company?) is t-e-e-n. I am told—nay, I am warned—in tones most ominous that Something Happens to the most pleasant youngster as he or she approaches the magic 13th birthday.

Take what happened to a friend of mine. (No names, please!) She has a 15-year-old son, right? Time for his annual physical, right? So she did what she always does. Made an appointment with his doctor. The pediatrician. Same doctor who has been looking after him since birth, right? Through immunizations, strep, kiddy diseases, you name it. No problem.

Or so she thought. Then she ran smack up against Murphy's Law of Adolescence: "Keep them off balance." The kid refused to go to the doctor.

But you need your annual physical, the mother said. Pleaded. Reasoned. Begged. Threatened. Nothing worked.

Listen, just put on your coat and let's move it and get this over with, said my friend the mother.

No way, said the son, as he handcuffed himself to his weightlifting bench.

Realizing she had lost the battle if not the war, she called in reinforcements. In other words, she called her husband at work and asked him to intervene.

He tried, he really did, but no dice. There was nothing to do but phone the pediatrician and cancel the appointment. Dr. Pediatrician, it must be noted, is a savvy lady who has seen all this before (although, perhaps, not with the added interest a pair of handcuffs and a weightlifting bench brought to the proceedings.)

Maybe it's time to take him to another doctor, Dr. Pediatrician said understandingly. Take him to your own physician, Dr. Internist. Or try Dr. Adolescent Specialist at the local health center.

Okay, said my friends the defeated parents. The kid uncuffed himself from the bench and they sat down to negotiate.

You have to have a physical, said the parents. You can choose which doctor you want, they bargained. Who will it be? Dr. Internist? Dr. Adolescent Specialist?

The kid chose, all right. Dr. Pediatrician.

After my friend told me the story, I whooped for a while, then shook my head and clucked, "Better you than me, honey!"

Then out of the clear blue came two unsettling thoughts. First, The Handcuff Kid will be driving next

142

year. Right here on the Commonwealth's highways, the same ones used by you and me and all those crazy drivers.

And second, I had a momentary sinking feeling. Now just suppose--what if--could it be--that my daughters would be adolescents themselves, one of these days?

Nah, I reassured myself, that won't happen here. My girls will be model teenagers, the type that glide around on stages and tell beauty contest judges that their hero is George Washington, their only hobby is baton twirling, and their favorite song is "When Irish Eyes Are Smiling."

Okay, there may be a few rough moments, but things are well in hand here. Can't you tell? Perfectly in control. My older daughter will clean up her room on demand. She will finish her homework the same week it is assigned (most of the time).

And the little one? Well, okay, I admit there are a few rough edges there that could use some smoothing. Okay, so she wore her sister's sneakers to church. So her sister's sneakers are a size 1, a tad big on Little One's size 9 feet. So she walked like Emmet Kelly. But hey, I have nine years until she's a teenager, and I'm sure I can whip her into shape by then.

If I could just figure out how to get her attention...

2005 update We have all survived Lisa's adolescence, which consisted of a lot of "teenaged angst." Mollie... well, Mollie makes me laugh, and it's a good thing. And as for The Handcuff Kid, he is now a pilot for a Major Airline. Be afraid. Be very afraid.

1987

Round and Round She Goes, She Stops, Owwww!

It is Sunday afternoon. I am sitting on a very narrow bench along the wall in a very large room lit by colored flashing lights. To say that the very walls vibrate from the pulsing rock music would be an understatement. I think my fillings are melting. Small children clomp past me. Smart alec teens glide past, dipping and swirling, cruising. Meanwhile, I am trying to put on a pair of high top shoes with wheels on the bottom. I am wishing my mommy were here to lace them up. I am going roller-skating.

It is not the first time I have ever been roller-skating, but it's close. I have not been roller-skating for about 25 years and then only once or twice at a little outdoor rink at the state park while everybody else was in the pool. I am questioning the wisdom of this excursion.

An announcer somewhere makes a long statement, not a single word of which is intelligible to me, but all of a sudden everyone on the floor is skating backwards. I am still on the bench. There isn't anything to hang onto, so I can't even get on my feet. This seemed like such a good idea at home last week.

A blast of cold air washes over my head. It is probably intended to cool my sweating brow. I am not sweating from exertion. I am still sitting on the bench.

"Mumble, mumble," the guy says, and everyone switches, skating backward in the opposite direction. Ray has gotten the girls' skates laced and is on his feet. There are many skaters whizzing around the rink. They are not my age. Nobody is old enough to vote. Most aren't old enough to drive. I feel inadequate. I wonder why we are not watching "Crocodile Dundee." I am 40 years old and I

144

am still sitting on the bench.

Lisa keeps telling me stories about people who fall down on roller-skating rinks and get run over, breaking important bones in their bodies. She is still hanging around the sidelines. Ray and Mollie slid into the crowd some time ago and I haven't seen them since. Lisa is the only one in the family who has roller-skated in recent memory. She has not skated yet today.

I am on my feet. I have found a half wall to hang onto. I am not going to let go. I remember my ice skating techniques. They do not work. I am shuffling around the rink now. The half wall ends abruptly but by then I am committed. There is (literally) no turning back. I look silly. I feel silly. I am also scared to death. Assorted parents are lined up along the half wall, on the other side. They are not wearing shoes with wheels. They are looking at me with pity.

Ray has ditched us and is gliding around the rink, hands in pockets. That's the difference, apparently, between city kids and county kids. We ice skate. They roller-skate. Life tends to divide along lines like that.

The lights go up again and the unintelligible announcer speaks at some length, after which a long line forms in the middle of the rink. They are going to do the Hokey Pokey. I am going to watch. When the songs says "put your left elbow in" at least a third of the skaters put their right elbows in. When it says "put your whole self in," some fall down. I sympathize.

Ray has worked up a sweat and goes off in search of a drink of water. Lisa is begging for money for the video games. Excruciatingly loud rock music fills the air. I cannot understand the lyrics. I am glad. I wish I couldn't hear the music, either.

There is one good thing about roller-skates. I am much taller when I am standing up, which isn't often. I do not fall because I do not try much to skate. Ray is crossing his skates, showing off. He looks great. I am

145

suitably impressed. He takes me around the rink a couple of times and I start to get the hang of it. We actually pass a couple of people. Unfortunately, the lights have been turned off and nobody can see us. We tell the kids to "sit right there." When we get back, both are gone and we spend the next 15 minutes looking for them.

The inevitable happens, I fall down. I am not injured. We head for the snack bar. I collapse into a chair and Ray has to get the drinks. I cannot be trusted to carry liquids. He suavely brings the drinks, goes back for napkins, wipes the table, turns to the trash can and falls to his knees in front of a garbage can. We can't stop laughing. People are watching us and edging away.

After the layover in the snack bar, I never quite get coordinated again. After a few more shaky turns around the rink, I am ready to throw in the towel. Ray and Mollie have already quit. Lisa is just getting started. Too bad.

I take my skates off. I am shorter. I am wiser. The kids want to come back next Sunday. We say let's wait at least until the pain goes away.

1989

A Spoonful of Sugar Wouldn't Hurt

It is Monday morning and Mollie is here with me. Vacation does not start until next week. Mollie is sick. Sort of. Since yesterday she has been sneezing and blowing her nose. If I had to work elsewhere this morning, I'd probably have dosed her up with something and sent her on her way with a box to tissues in her bag.

First thing this morning we checked Mollie's temperature. She does not have a fever. I am not surprised. She didn't have one last night when she insisted we check, either. At least, I don't think she has a fever. She clenched the thermometer between her teeth for a while, resisting all my efforts to get her to hold it beneath her tongue and keep her mouth shut, so that the thermometer might actually register somewhere near accurately. But the old "Mom's hand to forehead" technique tells me that she's "normal", and that will have to do.

This is good, because if she had a fever, I'd have to get her to take some aspirin or Tylenol (trademark). That is bad, because Mollie doesn't like to take medicine.

Well, to be perfectly fair about this, Mollie does take one particular kind of medicine, the Grape-Flavored Cold Medicine. The one that puts kids to sleep. It's always been one of my favorites because of that latter benefit—the kids sleep so I can.

Not that I'm about to get any sleep this Monday morning, you understand, because I do have work to do. I have two articles and two columns to write. I have some returned (read: rejected) pieces to submit to wiser editors. I have to call an industry association in Our Nation's Capital, where the person to whom I must speak will invariably be on the other phone. Then I have to go to the library for some special work, then to a meeting, then

147

back to the library for my regular evening shift. It is, in short, a typical Monday.

Except that now I have Mollie in tow.

Since we're out of Grape-Flavored-Etc., I try to get something different down Mollie. She doesn't like it. She actually lets me pour a teaspoon of the stuff into her mouth, but when it hits her taste buds, she spits it out. Down the front of her 'jammies, onto the floor. She then spits. And spits. And spits. It is great fun.

In fact, it reminds me not-so-fondly of the time about two years ago when she got tonsillitis and ear infections. After diagnosis, the doctor insisted Mollie take a little liquid Tylenol (trademark). Twenty minutes and three different samples later, the doctor headed for the airport to fly to Chicago wearing a skirt saturated with liquid Tylenol (trademark) in three different flavors. Getting Mollie's antibiotic down her the first time took an hour, but after that she apparently realized there was no way she could win.

That, as I said, was two years ago, and unfortunately, Mollie has forgotten that she can't win that one. It's Grape-Flavored-Etc. or nothing. I stick my finger in another bottle of liquid sniffles medicine. She won't taste it. I offer her a tiny red pill. She balks. I stir a teaspoon of another medicine into 12 ounces of grape juice. The taste nearly gags her.

She agrees, finally, to take the tiny red pill, but in three attempts, she comes close to choking to death (she says). She is not moved when I point out that the pill is about one-fourth the size of a chocolate chip, which she can swallow with great abandon.

I have to call the school's absence line to inform them that Mollie will be out. The instructions say I should estimate when she'll be back. I tell the Machine that Mollie may not be back at all, because, if she doesn't take the medicine, I'm going to kill her.

Happy Monday.

Finally, just when I have reached the very end of my rope, Mollie agrees to take the medicine I had dipped my finger into some time earlier. I scrub up, stick my finger in again, offer it. She likes it. I get a teaspoon down her.

This is just a skirmish victory, however. We now fight the "there's nothing to do" battle. I will not let her watch television. I suggest she read a book. She brings me one. I agree to read her a few pages. It's really a lovely book. I get interested and we finish it. Mollie colors several dozen post-season Easter egg pictures while I make some phone calls.

Finally I get to the computer. Mollie gets to the cat. The cat is carried past wearing Mollie's stretch slacks. I rescue the cat from the clothes hamper. I see the cat run for cover. The dog is curled up in a virtually inaccessible corner of my office. The dog is no fool. I discover that Mollie got the paper for her Easter egg pictures by unloading my printer.

Mollie turns the dust mop into a doll, wearing a wet dish towel, a baby dress, and a linen napkin. The fibers on the mop are too short and slippery to hold the barrettes she is trying to pin in the "doll" hair. As if there weren't several dozen dolls in her room just waiting to be dressed and fed.

Mollie makes another doll, this one from a paper towel roll with facial tissue hair. She attaches the hair with my last roll of tape.

It's a miracle. Mollie is cured. She's able to go back to school tomorrow.

No matter what.

2005 update: Mollie still insists on the Grape Flavored Etc., but at least she self-medicates now.

Let's NOT Get Physical

I will be the first to admit that my kids are couch potatoes. It's genetic. They get if from their father. Right. (No, I am *not* a couch potato. I'm a bookworm, and that's a whole other vegetable entirely.) So it's no surprise that physical education has been the bane of the Bracken existence for as long as I can remember.

Gym for Lisa was a disaster, partly because she was frankly in lousy shape and partly because she was so much smaller than the other kids. The class would get to tearing up and down the gym floor, all seemingly bearing down on her, and her first (and valid) impulse was to run for cover.

She protected herself by "forgetting" her gym clothes. It took me a while to catch on to this, since I was more engaged in letting her know how lucky she was to be taking gym in real shorts and tee shirts, since when I was young *yadda yadda yadda* — she had of course turned me off by then and completely missed my colorful description of the gym costume we had to wear: blue, baggy, designed to make even Madonna unattractive to teenaged boys with rampaging hormones. Very effective, too.

Lisa didn't want to hear about it. By the time I figured out how bad things were, she was scheduled to stay after school until the spring of 2001. (Since she was in the class of 1994, this was a clear indication of a major battle of wills.) Finally, in an attempt to meet Lisa halfway, the school administration agreed to send her to an evening adult aerobics class in lieu of gym. For the first time, Lisa wasn't griping about going to phys. ed. She even got a decent grade in it.

When she switched schools at the beginning of sophomore year, we didn't take any chances. We documented her health history to the phys. ed.

department and explained why it was important that she not take part in contact sports. No problem, said the school, and they made her a goalie! No contact...right! But she liked it and it seemed to be working out all right, so we let it go.

Then she took swimming and things started to go downhill. There aren't any goalies in swimming so it seemed appropriate to just turn her loose with the others. Wrong. I got a call one day to take her to the emergency room for a thumb x-ray after a mishap during lifesaving lessons. I knew then that it was a losing battle.

After that fiasco, she managed to avoid phys. ed. for a year, figuring she'd make up the final credits just before graduation. She signed on for weight-lifting classes senior year and actually liked them (well, maybe it was the fact that several of her good friends were sweating beside her...) Surgery precluded her finishing the semester and the requirement was waived so she could graduate. Whew!

One down, as the saying goes, and one to go. Mollie, it seems, is cut from the same cloth. While Lisa's gym problems didn't really escalate until freshman year, Mollie is nothing if not precocious. She has started the hassle two full years earlier. As was the case with Lisa, I didn't notice at first that anything was amiss.

But when we returned from our parents-only trip, it hit the you-know-what. We got home at midnight. When I got Mollie up the next morning at 6 a.m., she said, "I need sneakers."

"OK," I said, "but there's not much I can do about it right now." I mean, there are 24-hour drug stores and 24-hour restaurants and 24-hour supermarkets, but I'm not aware of any 24-hour shoe stores.

"I had to stay after school last week because I didn't have any and I have to stay after again today," she said, somewhat accusingly, I thought.

It didn't seem overly fair to me, but my brain was still on Caribbean time, and the adult in me tried to put myself in the teacher's place. His goal is to teach these kids the value of lifelong physical fitness. I don't envy him.

"Well, once you get home this afternoon, have your father take you to buy some sneakers," I said. I still hadn't had any caffeine.

By that evening, Mollie was all set with a snazzy new pair of sneakers. There was a bit of a tussle over the size of the shoes, but she insisted that the ones she bought, while tight, were a lot "cooler" than the larger ones her father favored. Shoes stretch. I figured we were home free.

I was wrong. The next evening, I asked her how it had gone.

I had to stay after school for gym," she reported. Huh? It seems that she was indeed wearing the aforementioned sneakers but had not changed into a tee shirt and therefore was deemed inappropriately dressed. "It was cold and I didn't want to change," she added.

I tried to put myself in the teacher's sneakers again. He's trying to teach hygiene. I can understand that. But this guy doesn't pay the kid's shampoo, soap, conditioner, hot water, etc., bills, or launder her towels. Trust me, she's one clean dude.

I thought about calling the school and telling the teacher that if he was trying to teach my kid a love of physical fitness, he was going about it all wrong. But before I got around to it, Mollie brought home her first report card of the year, and I dropped the whole thing.

Because she got her best grade in phys. ed., with a comment, "performs consistently well."

Go figure.

For richer, for poorer

The Inns and Outs of Gracious Living

Sooner or later it had to happen. So this weekend we took the Golden Arches crew to an inn for an Introduction to Gracious Living. This is the same outfit, remember, for whom a vacation is two weeks in a campground with a tepid shower every three days whether you need it or not. To them, soup grows on a Campbell's tree in pods called cans, to be prepared over some source of heat for dinner on nights when Mother works late. These people believe that no place is worth visiting if it doesn't allow dogs. Believe it or not, we took these people to an inn in Maine for a long weekend.

While our favorite inn is not an elegant mansion with suites and more servants than guests, it is a showcase for the owners' collection of cut glass and Delft china. Antiques are tastefully displayed throughout the renovated Depression-era boardinghouse. In short, it is not the kind of place a normal person would choose to take large dogs or small children.

We compromised. We left the dog home.

The inn is perched on a granite ledge above the causeway to a private Maine island accessible for guests' shore meanderings. There is a little beach (much larger when the tide is out) and rocks that trap tidal pools teeming with creatures that children under the age of 12 like to collect and take home so their mothers will become nauseous when doing the wash three weeks hence. I figured if the weather was good, the kids could for once spend as much time as they wanted on the beach making sand castles and collecting shells.

The weather cooperated beautifully. The kids didn't.

Daughter Number One wanted to spend the whole weekend in the living room reading Grimm's fairy tales. Our favorite two-year-old, on the other hand, just wanted to investigate the inn's kitchen. This little one, whose stamina is legendary among neighborhood babysitters, walked about six feet on our island hike, then demanded to be carried. It did not bode well. She and her father returned to the inn, along with her older sister, who had to go to the bathroom. I, on the other hand, had a wonderful tour of the island, found half a dozen nearly perfect sea urchin shells and shot an entire roll of film at the wrong speed.

A visit to this inn is like going to Grandmother's, and one is not required to "dress" for dinner, but we did so anyway. We started the meals by giving the children cranberry juice in wine glasses, causing other guests to eye us with some disfavor, the libation having the look of a particularly full-bodied red wine.

Saturday dinner at the inn is always lobster, steamed clams, and corn on the cob—not exactly fare for the well-dressed diner. No lobster bibs were available, either; actually, my kids until fairly recently thought a lobster was a fancy decoration on bibs one wears when eating spaghetti. Number Two Daughter got through her soup and some salad and then quit. Oh darn! (Hey, somebody had to eat her lobster.) Number One Daughter did eat a lobster. When she finished, she balanced a ravaged lobster body on top a pile of clam shells, from whence it fell to the well-polished wooden floor with a splat!

Sunday night there was a slight altercation over who would get the last piece of chocolate cream pie. (I won, but the booby prize was chocolate layer cake, so you need shed no tears for the loser.) We were the last to be served dessert because we were the last to finish eating—a consequence of leaving the table a number of times. The kid who has to be reminded at home to go to the bathroom made at least four trips during each and every meal at the inn. Then her father would wander off looking for her. Then her sister would go looking for both of them.

Thwarting Daughter Number Two's ambitions is asking for trouble. Noisy trouble. So whoever was left at the table usually had to take her outside, correct her, and give her a chance to cry it out of her system. Then, like a little parade, the Brackens would return to the dining room: Daughter Number One from the bathroom, father, Daughter Number Two, mother. We ate cold steak, cold lobster, cold corn on the cob...

Nor was breakfast without incident. The kid who sits in the kitchen at home for at least an hour consuming one breakfast after another had, at the inn, a table attention span of about 34 seconds. The pattern was repeated: cold pancakes, cold eggs, cold sausage...

Half the fun of going to an inn is in meeting the other guests. This weekend the inn boasted the usual gamut, including a newlywed couple (do they know how thin the walls are?) who looked askance at us, no doubt wondering if they ought to call the whole thing off; a set of grandparents who thought (or at least said) they missed their kids and ours were charming; and a Danish family with four handsome, polite, quiet, clean, bilingual children between the ages of one and 12, whose sole purpose in being there was probably to make us look bad.

Maybe there was another guest, too; the inn has a ghost named Peggy, who moves furniture around at night and steals shoelaces. I don't think she paid us a visit, but with the chaos, nobody would have noticed anyway.

Wheels of fortune

It's risky, I know. Getting rid of my old car automatically wipes out ideas for about a third of these columns. I have a way of getting mileage out of a vehicle that doesn't have anything to do with the distance it's driven.

But really. There comes a time when you have to bite the bullet, get out the checkbook, grovel at the bank, and take the plunge--choose your favorite cliché.

The time had come. My ego isn't tied up in my car, so I can overlook a lot, but some equipment I consider standard in a viable vehicle. Like doors. Or, to be more specific, doors that work. Oh, sure, the wagon had five doors, counting the cargo gate, but when I started counting the ones that really worked right, I could do it on one finger. And that admirable door happened to be the aforementioned cargo gate. Okay, one door (passenger rear) did still open from the outside, but it didn't close very well, flying open on more than one occasion when I went around a corner just right.

I didn't mind when the passenger front door quit, or even the driver rear. Losing the driver door, however, was a blow. But hey, I'm adaptable. So I would leave the window open and just reach inside when I wanted to open the door. The latch still worked from the inside. No problem.

This worked fine all summer, when the weather was clear and warm and the garage door functioned as it should. But fall came, and a touch of winter, and with that seasonal change came some quirks. Like the garage door slipped its hinges and the repair person, who said he'd be here at 5 on Friday, neglected to mention which week. Or year.

So okay, I parked the car outside. When the weather was good, I left the driver window open. When it wasn't, I climbed in the passenger rear door, crawled halfway over the front seat to open the front passenger door, hiked back out and slid across the seat--all the while grateful that we were past the infant seat stage.

Then a bunch of things happened at once. The speedometer quit working in August, so I could never figure out if I was courting trouble or not. With it went the odometer, at 173,982 miles. The windshield developed a crack that grew almost perceptibly each day. The insurance company would have replaced the glass, but that meant we would lose the inspection sticker, which the gas station wouldn't reissue unless we got the exhaust leak fixed.

Even with all that, I was willing to try to get the car through the winter. I figured that if I had to make any long business trips, I would just rent a car for a day or two. But the oil leak clinched it. Driving more than a couple of miles was asking for puffs of smoke from under the hood.

Ray tried to talk me into buying a 15-year-old car. But it didn't make sense to buy something somebody else might have already driven into the ground, when I could do that just fine myself, thanks very much.

We had a new car once. It was 1972, and we bought a medium-sized sedan for $2932. As of this week, we have another new car, and it cost three times as much for about half the car. My new car only has two doors (plus the hatchback)--which doesn't sound like much for a family car, until you consider that it's still twice as many functioning doors as we ended up with on the wagon.

We could have bought something used from a private party, I suppose, but that would have left us with our old station wagon--a car that I would not sell to a friend. Or a stranger, either. But I had no hesitation in dumping it on the dealer. The salesman said he'd allow us a trade-in of $874 for the wagon. I'm guessing we could have gotten $1000 discount for NOT trading in the wagon, but I don't want to know for sure.

We picked up the car the other day. It's a standard shift, so I was a little apprehensive about relearning how to drive, but Ray was willing to remind me. This means that when he finally let me drive "my" car (all the way home from the convenience store), he kept yelling, "More gas! Give it more gas!

When we bought the other new car, in 1972, we noticed a couple of nicks in the paint. No problem, the dealer said--and handed us a little bottle of paint, not unlike fingernail polish. When we picked up this new car, the salesman went over the whole finish with us and spotted a tiny chip in the hood paint. For three times as much money, you apparently get three times as much service--the car goes to the body shop for two days.

This morning, with all of 106.2 miles on the odometer, I cleaned out the car for the first time. I found one Fruit Fragrance pen, a child's purse, a paper plate turkey Kindergarten project, two pairs of socks, and four cardboard bits of varying sizes from a snack wrapper.

So in case you're worried that I will run out of things to write about, never fear. We didn't trade in the kids.

2005 update: We drove that vehicle, dubbed the Clown Car for its abilities to hold unbelievable quantities of luggage, groceries, and junk, not to mention kids and pets, for at least 150,000 miles until Ray had a too-close encounter with another car at the Concord Rotary. We do get our automotive money's worth.

For better, for worse

The Clothes They Wore

A few weeks ago I saw an article in the paper about a child being taken from her parents' custody and being made a ward of the state. The reason: neglect. The evidence: the kid was found sitting in an 85 degree apartment, wearing a heavy sweater, long slacks and a wool hat.

After reading that, you can bet I looked furtively over my shoulder, taking mental inventory of my kids' outfits. If that's neglect, my girls have it, too. But they brought it on themselves.

You know how Saturday was warm and humid? Mollie started the day in a sundress (size 3) and panties, no shoes or socks. So far so good, right? Somewhere around noon, I think it was, she changed into a size 2 winter pajama top with ripped sleeves and a pair of size 8 summer baby doll pajama bottoms. Ray didn't see anything wrong with the outfit (or the fact that she was parading down the sidewalk wearing it); tops and bottoms were both pink, he said, so they matched well enough.

What she was doing on the sidewalk, you understand, was pushing an empty carriage up and down the street, talking a blue streak to the thin air and waving to everyone who passed. Believe me, she looked like she hasn't got both oars in the water.

Now Lisa, on the other hand, got up on the hot morning and put on a pair of pink dungarees and a bright yellow sweater. Wool. Long sleeved. I'll say one thing, you wouldn't lose her in a dark room. And summer doesn't seem to bother her, I'll give you that. I practically faint with heat prostration just looking at her, but she's as cool as diamonds on ice.

I suppose I shouldn't complain. For the most part, the girls look pretty good. My friend June has a cartoon showing two kids. One has perfectly combed hair, a fancy dress, socks, shoes, you name it; the other one has hair not unlike a plate of spaghetti, a dress with hem hanging and buttons missing, unmatched socks falling around her ankles. The caption: Which Child Has the Working Mother.

My kids have a working mother, so I knew the answer to that one. They usually go around looking like a pair of unmade beds. But I got an unexpected check from a California newspaper and blew part of it on summer haircuts for the girls. They look really cute, like somebody cares. I even spent half a day sorting clothes in their room so they would have summer things to wear in the summer. In the process, I packed things that don't fit either of them (some haven't fit anybody who lives here for a couple of years) for storage. I mean, I'm trying, right?

So Sunday afternoon, Lisa and Mollie decided they wanted pony tails. Did they want pony tails when they both had tresses straggling down their backs? Heck, no! They want pony tails now, when they have about 3" of hair.

Then there are the socks. I am tempted to quit washing socks, just throw them away when they get too dirty to be seen in. (That point, of course, would be reached a lot sooner for Mollie, who insists on wearing only white socks, and won't put them in the wash until they look like they've been on a mud wrestler; Lisa, on the other hand, will change her socks twice before breakfast.) Think of the aggravation I'd save by just tossing out the socks instead of trying to hang onto the pink one until its mate comes out of the wash a month later. Heck, the savings in Valium alone would pay for new socks.

But I digress. The wardrobe problem came to a head when Ray was going to run errands. Mollie insisted on going along—hysterically. Okay, he said, but put on some shoes. The kid owns white patent leather shoes, blue sneakers and red sneakers. What did she put on? A red Velcro sandal, about size seven. And a blue flip-flop, maybe size twelve. Both lefts.

The fellow at the gas station, spotting the footwear, said to Ray, "Remind me not to take you along when I go to buy shoes."

Or socks, either, I would imagine. She was wearing white socks, sure, but one had a blue band and the other a red one.

You might think I therefore despair of the time I spent sorting out their wardrobes, putting the red check shorts with the matching top, stowing the snowsuits and mittens, tucking the sundresses in the most accessible drawer.

Well, you'd be wrong. I know perfectly well that those shorts and halter tops will get plenty of wear—next January.

2005 update: Mollie and shoes—well, let's just say we call her Imelda Bracken. She does wear them in matching pairs, though.

Caribbean Departure

OK, we had our passports and had given some thought to our wardrobe for our Caribbean vacation. Understand, I'm not at my best when packing for a trip. With us, that usually means not only clothes, but also camping stuff, food, and all the rest. This time would be different. Just Ray and me. Beachside villa, catered meals, lapping waves. This time, I was going to be pampered. This time would be a piece of cake.

Wrong. I hadn't even started the dreaded ironing before things started to get weird.

I am a list person, and had made a long list of stuff that had to be done. It was Election Day, so the top thing was to vote. When I got home from work, all of us eligible to vote (that's three now...) looked all over the house for one of those sample ballots to speed things up in the polling booth. We finally found one, agreed to disagree (and cancel each other's votes) on some of the referenda, went down to the high school gym, stood in line, did our civic duty (and earned griping rights for the next four years), then headed for a pizza place for a quick supper.

The pizza place was playing hard rock. Very loud hard rock. The girls didn't even like the particular songs; Lisa kept saying, as each one painfully started, "Oh, I hate this song!" Ray and I, need I say it, hated 'em all. We sat there, trying not to think about how slow the kitchen was and how much we still had to do, not to mention how early 5 a.m. was going to seem.

As we were sitting there, Lisa said casually, "Oh, did I tell you the travel agency called? Well, no, as a matter of fact, she hadn't. And the message? "It was something about a delay or technical difficulties. Dougie took the message."

165

Dougie? Dougie is the kid next door. He's a nice kid and we like him, but I have spent the past 15 years or so trying to teach my kids to take messages or at least leave the answering machine on. Dougie missed out on that.

"Well," Lisa reported, "he said something about the plane being maybe delayed or the flight canceled or something about technical difficulties." Technical difficulties? Who wants to hear about technical difficulties regarding an airplane they're about to board?

Lisa went to a pay phone and called Dougie for further details. There weren't any. By then, the travel agency had been closed for at least two hours. I'm not sure how I ate a salad and a piece of pizza with my teeth clenched, but I assure you, nobody was allowed to linger. At home, I called the airline. They didn't know of any problems.

I called the trip packager. They didn't know of any problems.

So I called the travel agent at home. There was nothing about flight cancellations or delays. There was nothing about technical difficulties. Someone just thought we hadn't picked up our tickets, which we had.

I tried to relax after that, I really did, but let's face it. You can do stuff to your own kids, like threaten not to bring them back a t-shirt if they mess up important phone messages, but you can't do that with the neighbors.

By then I was on a roll. It was not a pretty sight. Even mild-mannered Dougie had had enough and went home to avoid being caught up by the cranky dervish I had become. We finally got things packed and hit the sack. Try sleeping sometime while visions of "technical difficulties" dance in your head. Right.

In the morning things started going better, and I could see the humor in the situation. Like the guy at airport security who had an entire basin of metal he'd had to remove to pass trough the gate: bracelets, neck chains, chain link belt, who knows what else. All I could think was, if he fell into a full tub of anything while dressed, he didn't have a chance. Another guy (middle-aged and old enough to know better) usurped an entire overhead compartment on the plane with a boom box the size of Rhode Island. Luckily, he left it there for the flight, although I didn't envy anyone within six blocks of his final destination.

We were expecting a three-and-a-half hour layover in the San Juan airport, but I suggested that we try to get an earlier flight. The airline put us on standby, and I was excited. We were almost there, and no problems, so far.

We were called at the last minute and boarded a shuttle bus out to the far reaches of the airport to get on our plane. A man sharing the shuttle wondered if we were driving to Tortola instead. It did seem like a long way out, but I think it was mostly driving in circles for effect.

We arrived at tiny, un-air-conditioned Beef Island International Airport on Tortola after a flight of 27 minutes without a hint of "technical difficulties." I won't say it was a quickie, but the in-flight snack consisted of the attendant passing down the aisle with a basket of mints.

We arrived.

Our luggage, naturally, did not.

'Sounds of silence' have gone to the dogs

Ah, summertime, and the windows are open. Things have been mercifully quiet here for the most part, especially when compared to the summers of the school construction across the street with all the big truck traffic braking 30 feet from our front door. Even sitting on the back porch didn't blunt that skreeeeeeeking much.

Note I said it's quiet *for the most part.* The other part concerns Man's Best Friend. Don't get me wrong — some of my favorite breathing creatures have had four paws and a wagging tail. Over our three decades on Goldsmith Street, we have made a home for three dogs at various times; unlike cats, canines come one at a time to our house. Let's face it — compared to felines, dogs are high maintenance.

And noisy. Long after dogs have learned (hopefully) to leave the garbage alone and (hopefully) to use the big outdoors as a potty and to do all manner of tricks like catch and fetch for hours on end, there is still that bark. I know there are breeds that don't bark, but that seems just too weird. Our first dog, Sheba, was not much of a barker; she was a digger though, which seems to be a tradeoff. Our second dog, Whiskers, who shared this space with us half of our years here, didn't bark all that much either, but she was too busy tearing up the furniture to note outside activity that should be brought to our attention.

And now there's Sandy. She will never reach the pinnacle of Barking Dogdom, a record currently held by our neighbor's Labrador retriever, Bo. Bo has calmed down a lot, but for many, many months he did nothing but bark — day and night, constantly. That dog has stamina! We dubbed him Bob's Barker, after his then-owner. It was almost tolerable for us, living across the street and with our bedroom on the back side of the house, but for the next-door folks, sleeping (or trying to) maybe 50 yards from his outdoor run, the noise was infuriating. Dire threats were made, although probably not to the dog's owner.

Eventually Bo began to sport a jaunty new collar with a box attached. Turns out that's a special device to train dogs, mostly painlessly unless they're slow learners, not to bark. The collars, I understand, react to the motion of the dog's vocal chords, giving a little electrical shock at each bark. It sounded sort of medieval torture-like, except that the alternative was much less pleasant and involved unthinkable and irreversible alterations to the dog's anatomy. Whatever, Bo stopped barking. That all happened several years ago and today we hear him only rarely and briefly.

So when Sandy came to live with us, I was aware of potential cures for her barking. She does not bark for hours on end, unless she's tied in the back yard, which we simply stopped doing after a couple of tries. (Someone here is a fast learner; I'm just not sure it's Sandy. Or maybe it is?) I would characterize her more as a stealth barker. Everything is quiet and peaceful, when all of a sudden: Wham! Sandy is tearing from room to room, barking madly, and her humans are grasping at their chests in alarm.

Her reasons are generally clear — at least to her. People passing on Goldsmith Street rate a few minutes' barking from at least two windows in different rooms. Depending on their route, they might merit extra barks from a third room and window.

Dogs passing on Goldsmith Street get the same treatment, although it can be prolonged with back-and-forth shifts as the unleashed dogs wander around the neighborhood.

The worst, though, is the indoor barking in response to imagined threats. Like the cats. Ziggy is the primary recipient of this behavior, since he is the only cat who spends much time outdoors. After a while, he will repair to the screened porch, curl up on a cushioned chair and sleep. The ever-alert Sandy will notice this and launch into high gear, yipping and yapping and yowling, as if to say, "Holy moly! Look! There's a cat out there! Look, everybody, there's a cat out there! Look! Look! Cat!"

After some Bracken escorts the cat from the porch past the yawning maw of the dog, upstairs to safety, Sandy will settle down, exhausted, to rest up, usually on an upholstered chair in the living room. Meanwhile, Ziggy will use the litter box (for this he comes inside...), have a bite to eat, get a drink of water, and let himself back out onto the upstairs deck, from whence he ventures up to the roof, down to the lawn, and the process repeats itself. Before long, Ziggy will be sleeping on the porch and Sandy will be slavering at the porch door, yipping and yowling and yapping as if to say, "Holy, moly! Look! There's a cat out there! Look, everybody, there's a cat out there! Look! Look! Cat!"

Sandy also serves as doorbell, since our doors lack such amenities. Luckily she has a slightly different and more sustained bark that means "Hey! Who's out there? Somebody, come see who's at the door!" She uses this version when people approach our door but decline to knock — like the delivery people who leave boxes on the stoop, or maybe even any approaching burglars put off by the presence of the obviously fierce dog inside.

The trick is to encourage timely barking (like when somebody with a pellet gun uses parked cars as a target in a Littleton version of drive-by shooting) but discourage annoyance barking (like when nobody will throw the tennis ball for the hundredth time).

We may have a plan.

(To be continued...)

2000

Hark! Hark! The dogs do bark

Well, here it is summer. In winter we hibernate, close our houses, hide within. In summer, we open those windows and those doors and let the neighbors hear how we really live. In our case, that means occasional arguments, loud television programs, and Sandy the ever beloved barking dog.

As she tears from room to room, woofing and yelping, scratching the floors with her claws, sliding around corners, her voice level probably rivals a jet at takeoff. Occasionally Sandy and Bo, the Neighbor's Barker, get into duets. One of them barks. The other, wondering what s/he's missing, picks up the refrain. Pretty soon they're exchanging recipes or whatever it is that dogs "talk" about when they're not alerting their families to the presence of cats or mail carriers.

This being animal-crazy Littleton, Sandy and Bo form but a minority of neighborhood dogs. Some of the others are free to wander around at will (*Can you say leash law?*), while others are kept at home or only appear on the sidewalk leashed, their passage noted by the canine chorus that greets them. They have also been known to join the barking, just for the fun of it.

So what happens is, say Dog A starts barking at a squirrel. Luckily, the other dogs are napping or otherwise occupied, but Dog A keeps it up long enough for Neighbor B to snap. "Shut the #$%^&*&^%% up!" shouts Neighbor B. Dog A, monetarily distracted, stops barking. However, Dog B, Dog C and Dog D hear the shout and find it necessary to respond. And the bark goes on.

Or maybe not. Friends of ours in another town, whose parenting and pet-owning paths have pretty much paralleled our own, are fighting the same battle. They have three dogs at the moment, which is why when a homeless puppy was offered to them, they turned it down. Instead the puppy went to some friend of a friend of a

171

friend. The puppy came with stuff including one of those no-bark collars. The new owners, sure of their doggy training skills, took only the animal, assuring one and all that the collar would not be necessary, thank you very much. The other accouterments were divided among various good homes. Our friends got the no-bark collar.

It was delivered one summer evening while their 20-something son and his friends were in the driveway sampling the delights of hops and malt. The no-barking collar was too good to pass up. They took turns trying it on and barking. They pronounced it quite effective, especially with the four-level power at top charge.

I happened to be at their house a day or so later when my friend decided to test the collar on their barking dog. Of their three canines, one is especially vocal, more so since her aging joints have limited her mobility and made barking her main pleasure in life. Her owners had tried the pennies-in-an-empty can trick and all the rest of the stuff they learned through their addiction to the vet shows on the cable channel Animal Planet. The dog still barked.

My friend put the collar on the dog. We sat back in poolside chairs to wait. The dog barked about the collar. The dog barked about the chairs. The dog barked about the pool. The dog barked about my friend and probably about me. The collar had absolutely no effect. Probably because the dog is a Samoyed with several inches of thick, long fur protecting her neck and body-- attributes more useful on the Iditarod trail than a Massachusetts summer, but what can you do? The collar was a failure.

When I left that day, I had the collar. When Sandy started barking the next day, a daughter put it on the dog's neck Sandy didn't much like the feel of the collar but had no difficulty barking around it. Once it was adjusted properly, though, to stay in place against her throat, the collar had an obvious effect. Sandy would bark once, let out a light yelp, and shut up. Ray would feel sorry for her, remove it, I would suggest that the power level be adjusted, and so forth.

I think we went around this circle three or four times, proving to me that certain members of my family are demonstrably less trainable than the dog. Right about then my friend called and asked for the collar back.

Seems the puppy's new owners had, in just a few days, earned the enmity of their neighbors and received visits from both the police and the dog officer, all complaining about the barking.

So the current score is: Dog 1, Collar (and humans) 0.

Why am I not surprised?

2005 update: Sandy still barks. Should anyone want to comment about her meanderings around the neighborhood sans leashed owner in tow, it's the man of the house who needs to be trained.

2001

As Popeye says, 'I Yam who I Yam.'

Well it's just happened again. At the supermarket I smiled at a cute little tyke, maybe 3 years old, who turned to her mother and said, loudly, "Mommy, that lady has a fat tummy!"

I never know quite how to respond to that, so I don't say anything. I mean, it's the truth, of course, but I'm tempted to reply, "Yes, but I'm not rude." We are the Final Frontier of Discrimination. We are the Fat.

People seem to think it's OK to "belittle" the Fat, to expect the worst of us. Have you seen pictures of Christopher Reardon and Michael Skakel? How about the guy who went ballistic at his work place last year and blew away some co-workers? Fat, all of them.

I can't really blame anyone who has that attitude. I was raised with the notion that being fat was the worst thing in the world. In my family alcoholism, emotional abuse, quitting jobs regularly, and sexual abuse were apparently okay, since nothing was ever said about it. But boy! Was I constantly reminded that I was – I am – fat.

This, of course, after being "fed" the notion that dinner plates should be cleaned no matter how much food had been piled on them. Children were starving in China, and by George, I had better eat all that liver and onions. I never did figure out how my eating too much spaghetti would keep a child in China from an awful death, but I was nothing if not dutiful, so I ate every bite.

As a result I have battled the bulge for the past forty-five years, and the bulge usually wins. My most recent attempt to pare off the pounds and inches was wildly successful.I did enjoy buying all new clothes and accepting compliments on my good looks. But I eventually realized that in order to be thin, I had to spend all my free waking hours working on it. I went to work

174

and watched my weight. That was it. I dropped off all my committees and canceled commitments. I planned every bite I ate. I talked all the time about what I was and was not eating. If I wasn't eating, I was on the phone or at meetings trying to get and stay thin.

In short, I did not have a life. Sure, I want to be thin, but I also want to take part in writers' groups, to work on church committees, to go places with friends.

I got my life back, along with thunder thighs and a big butt. Not to mention, as the supermarket tyke did, my fat tummy. I try to adopt Camryn Manheim's attitude; she's the actress who wrote the book, *Wake Up, I'm Fat.* I do pretty well most of the time; I exercise regularly, I am kind to strangers, I drive politely, I do both of my jobs well, I am tactful, I take in stray cats, I have many good friends, I've been married to the same man for 31 years, I've raised two independent young women, and I don't kick the dog. But still, the most important thing about me seems to be, I am Fat.

One big issue seems to be the amount of space we fatties take up in airplanes. We do fill our seats and some of us a bit more. But personally I'd rather sit next to a polite fat person than a drunk or a bore or one of those dopes who fills all the overhead compartments with a complete household worth of goods because the rules don't apply to them. Give me John Goodman over Woody Allen any day.

I was especially taken aback with the little girl's comment this morning because I had had such a struggle zipping my jeans after a summer of shorts that I was feeling both squashed flat, and since I was buying lots of low-fat food, quite virtuous.

So, little girl, wherever you are, I would like you to know that I write stories for children, help them with their homework, provide toys for them while their parents surf the web at the library, and have a great sense of humor.

Given all that, why do I feel so bad about myself just because I'm fat? Years of therapy, and I still don't know.

In sadness and in joy

Back with 'That old gang of mine'

It was a Sunday afternoon and the people gathered at the big old hilltop farmhouse had driven in from the seacoast region and from the next state. After all those Christmas notes ending we-must-get-together-sometime, we had done it. The old college theater gang (or at least part of it) was together again.

I hadn't seen Ozzie since 1967, although I had heard of her now and again from the others. Ozzie, after an odyssey that took her from New Hampshire to Japan and Germany and back, through a brief marriage to will-o-the-wisp Pete and a stint with a rock band, has evolved into Mary Anne, an elementary school readiness teacher with two kids and a former pet-shop-owner husband.

We had gotten together with the other two couples in the recent past, not for a couple of years, now, but enough to know that the fellow we had fondly called Monkey is a store owner and father of four. Kids look at you funny when you call their father Monkey. So it's time to become Dick. In what must be something of a record, he's still happily married to his high school sweetheart, Vicky. Of their four kids, they refer to the older as the first generation (aged 15 and 10) and the younger as the second generation(3 and 4).

Kris is still singing and her husband John is directing community theater, two of the lucky ones who have kept the dream alive even if it doesn't put bread on the table. In real life, John--crazy, wacky John--is, of all things, a police dispatcher. As Dick commented, people in John's town can skip cable TV and get a police scanner to tune in the best show in town.

Okay, Kris works at the university and John's a cop, but their friends know by now to open their Christmas cards away from the kids' prying eyes. They are the only couple I know who send holiday greetings that should be sent in a plain brown wrapper. I mean, how many people do you know whose family pet was obtained as a result of a "large vermin" report from the Howard Johnson's ladies' room? They named the errant guinea pig, saved from certain death at the hands of the SWAT team, Squeaky.

Getting together in the farmhouse, we spent the first hour or so introducing everybody.

"This is Joe."

"Joe, Ray."

And so forth. The trickiest to sort out were the kids. Of the 10 of them, there were two Lisas and an Alicia. There were four fourth graders and one six-year-old miffed because there was nobody her age to play with. It sounded a lot like one of those logic problems: If Ben is Amy's brother and Tim was the last to be potty-trained, who owns Patches the goat?

Mollie, naturally, threw a monkey (not Dick) wrench into the proceedings. She's been having an identity crisis lately. So when I said, "This is Mollie," she of course replied, "No, I'm Sarah." That brought the number of Sarahs up to two.

To further confuse the issue, Mollie wandered into the dining room after a while and asked, "Where's Kate?" After a moment's silence while the grownups mentally ran down the cast of characters, someone risked being accused of senility to ask, "Who's Kate?" (There was no Kate.)

There were kids in and out, kids eating, kids playing, but fortunately, no kids fighting. When one of the fourth graders shook a can of soda and then opened it, the resulting explosion was fortunately confined to a bathroom sink; coming in at the tail end of the conversation to hear that there was no mess to clean up, one mother leaped to the usual conclusion and asked, "Who threw up?"

For several hours we asked whatever-happened-to so-and-so, found out who of the rest of the gang is living on a yacht in Hawaii, who is earning a living in the theater, who we saw on television, and who's come out of the closet.

After half an hour of struggle with what the stores fondly call winter outerwear, the kids went sledding. Mollie (or was it Sarah), still wearing her sister's too-big sneakers, ended up with soaked feet, and Tracy was annoyed because nobody would let her direct traffic.

As the afternoon slipped into evening, the party's finale featured two forty-year-old men sliding down the hill, a yowling blue tick hound named Blue in hot pursuit. Gee, it was such fun, maybe somebody should make a movie about it. The reunion of some college friends. Have them go sledding. Call it "The Big Chill."

2005 update: We just had another reunion, this one with Martha, Bob and Kathy added. We spent several hours catching up; the news, as we age, is about grandchildren, retirement, family illnesses, and deaths—who died and who turned up at the funeral. I remind my children that in this case, "old" refers to the friendship, not the people.

Here and there: a study in contrasts

Sunday morning 7:30 a.m. The sun is back, the jaunty breeze tossing the trees. The week of rain is behind us, the lawn ripe for another mower attack. I sit on the new porch, my feet up on the comfortable chaise lounge, a cup of tea at my side. I open the Sunday paper and begin to read.

Beijing. The paper has a reporter's diary of the horrible week in China. Unthinkable. Tragic. Mesmerizing.

An occasional car passes on Goldsmith Street. Later the traffic will be heavier, the noise more annoying, but for now I listen to the rustle of the leaves and the birds singing in the maple tree.

Beijing. An occasional tank rumbles through the streets and lanes near Tiananmen Square. The students and the rebellious workers have been routed. Later the traffic will be heavier as armored personnel carriers fill the streets with soldiers. But not as many soldiers as there were students last week — maybe even millions of them. There are merely thousands of soldiers. That is enough.

Now and then someone walks down the street, enjoying the bright clean morning air and the flash of the leaves in the sunlight.

Beijing. Students run from the splatter of assault rifle fire, perhaps slipping on the blood spilled by their wounded and dying comrades.

Someone's dog ambles into the street. Cars slow to let him pass.

Beijing. Heaps of bicycle racks and burned-out vehicles block the intersections. The army smashes through.

A bicycle flashes by as someone rides into the pleasant day on my street.

Beijing. Rickshaw bicycles are makeshift ambulances as dying Chinese are hurried to hospitals already full with victims.

I sip my cup of tea, now cooling as the morning advances.

Beijing. Reporters sit at a hotel, drinking beer, taking cover when the bullets fly too close.

Midweek, a young Chinese mother had come to the library and asked in halting English for information on our government — federal, state, local. She is applying for U.S. citizenship. As she reads the books I have found for her, her young daughters play in the children's room. I wish her well.

Beijing. The reporter dives for cover in a bush as troops shoot wildly at anything and nothing. A teenaged student finds refuge in the same bush. They have no common language but fear. They hold hands, then help each other up when the danger is past. They dash off in their separate ways. The girl must stay. The reporter may leave.

I think about 1970. May 4, the day I had my last graduate class. This day is forever etched in my memory — classes canceled because of the Kent State shootings half a country away in Ohio. The frightened National Guard soldiers killed four demonstrators, and the administration is afraid we Boston students will take to the barricades in protest. There is little to fear from my fellow library science colleagues.

Beijing. The reporter speaks with a professor who has cast his lot with the students. They hear noise. What is that, the professor asks. Gunfire, the reporter replies. No, no, says the professor, they are trying to scare us with firecrackers, but firecrackers will never stop us. A world away from Kent State and 19 years. How may are dead? 400? How many will die in the crackdown? 4000? How many will the Chinese government sacrifice to quell the revolt? Four million?

I think about the sunny morning a few weeks ago, Memorial Day, when we turned out to remember those who have fought for the democracy we so take for granted. We gathered around the monuments on the Common — not by the millions, certainly, but by the hundreds — a respectable crowd for a lovely long and lazy weekend.

Beijing. The foam and plaster replica of the Statue of Liberty, the "Goddess of Democracy," standing as a symbol above the unarmed students in Tiananmen Square is blown apart and mowed down as the crowd is blown apart, mowed down. As the soldiers destroyed China's past in the Cultural Revolution, are they now prepared to destroy their future as well?

Some of the passing cars on Goldsmith Street have full luggage racks on the roof and tow trailers behind. The weekend campers are wandering home.

Beijing. The vehicles leaving the city are laden with passengers, piled high with suitcases. The people are fleeing the capital, fleeing the wrath of the government, fleeing the army's bullets. The soldiers chant, "We love the people. We love the people," as they fire into the peacefully demonstrating crowds.

My daughters sleep peacefully under colorful quilts I have made for them.

Beijing. A mother has come to the makeshift morgue to take her son's body away. Tell the people, she says to the reporter, he died for China.

I listen to my two children awaken, get breakfast, squabble, dress for Children's Sunday at church. There will be a picnic afterwards. I think about the grieving Chinese mother and wonder if under her country's "one child" policy she has lost her immortality.

I weep for her.

2005 update: This piece won first place in the National Newspaper Association "best column" competition.

183

Greetings from Tinsel Town

Don't get me wrong — I love Christmas. I love the secrets and the carols (well, maybe except for Nat King Cole singing "O Tannenbaum" in lousy German). I love the lights twinkling through lightly sifting snow.

I love the advent services and the advent calendar and the advent candles. I love trying to find just the right gift for everyone on my list — and I love it even better when I can afford it. I love having Christmas in our own home midweek because then I get a stocking full of goodies. I've been good — no coal for me.

I love getting cards and letters from people I care about and hear from once a year. I love getting handmade cards from my kids with heartfelt messages like the one on my birthday:

"Though you're old, you're still kickin'
Yes, you're no spring chicken.
Don't feel sad, don't feel blue.
'Cause everyone still loves you.
Roses are red, violets are blue
Happy Birthday to skinny you."

Or the one on Thanksgiving expressing gratitude for parents, sister (reluctantly) and the fact that we hadn't put her in an orphanage.

I love the parties where I get kissed by all the guys, even when there's no mistletoe.

I love the church services, especially the family one on Christmas Eve where everyone brings all the kids, who are totally off the wall with excitement and couldn't sit quietly for 15 seconds, let alone an hour. Mother is still in awe at the minister's unflappable ability to raise his voice above the pandemonium.

I love making gifts and having an excuse to knit for hours on end while listening to a good book on tape with my feet up and the cat purring in my lap.

I love the holiday spirit that led my niece, who moved West with no forwarding address several years ago, to call with her address and phone number.

I love trudging through the New Hampshire woods with a big bunch of family, looking for perfect Christmas trees. I love the smell of the fresh-cut balsam and the cinnamon cookies and the roasting turkey and the hollyberry candles.

I don't mind never being able to find the scissors or the tape and I don't mind cleaning bits of ribbon and rolls of wrapping paper every time I set the table for dinner.

I don't mind shopping in the crowds. I don't mind walking twice as far from my car parked in the next county from the mall. I don't mind waiting in long checkout lines as clerks muddle through their first day on the job and screw up every single transaction, requiring constant calls to the harassed manager, who is invariably at lunch.

I don't even mind having to untangle all the light strings and the ornament hooks. I don't mind putting a sheet under the tree, then replacing it every time I've left the house because the dog drags it out for a comfy bed whenever our backs are turned.

So what's the problem? It's this darned tinsel, I mean, I can't imagine a Christmas tree without tinsel, but the stuff is more invasive than the sands in Saudi Arabia. It's everywhere.

Tinsel is Christmas. Tinsel is the final touch — the shimmery icicles to be hung lovingly, strand by clingy strand, on each tiny branch and bough, right?

Wrong. Unfortunately, as I opened the box of tinsel that I'd bought over Ray's objections (for some reason, he's anti-tinsel), the phone rang and I passed the box to Mollie. By the time I got back from the wrong number call, Mollie was finished. And so was the tree. There were maybe eight clumps of tinsel on the tree, each with about 250 strands. (The box said 2000 stands, and I'm willing to take their word for it.) It looked like the work of a giant spider on LSD.

I tried to separate the stands but in the 30 seconds they'd fused into an impossible tangle. Of course, the tinsel doesn't just sit there, clumps or no. It migrates. Within an hour there was tinsel on the cat, tinsel on the dog, tinsel on lampshades, tinsel in the rabbit cage, tinsel in the dishwasher, and tinsel in Ray's beard. Heck, there's still tinsel on the front railing from *last year's* tree.

The curious thing about tinsel is its remarkable ability to reproduce. From those 2000 original strands there are now several hundred thousand pieces on the living room carpet alone, not to mention a lifetime supply in such outposts as the garage and the cat's litter box.

When you think about it, it's amazing stuff, tinsel. It flies better than paper airplanes, sticks better than scotch tape, doesn't burn, lasts longer than a paycheck, and multiplies likes rabbits.

Pretty durable stuff, indeed. Must be made of fruitcake.

2005 update: A few years ago we switched to substantial twisty aluminum reusable "tinsel" icicles. Last I looked, one of them was on the garage steps.

How to prepare for a family emergency

I am going to stray a little from my usual column topic to give all my readers some advice. We read all the time about home fire drills, escape ladders, making a household inventory, backing up all the important computer stuff on discs stored somewhere outside the house or office, and keeping important documents in a fireproof yet accessible box. I would like to report that I have all that under control, but I'd be lying. I did insist on buying escape ladders for each of the girls' bedrooms, but in the event they were needed, I would bet my eyeteeth that nobody could find them, let alone sling them out the window and get away safely.

I don't remember, however, ever hearing about preparing for medical emergencies except to learn CPR, keep first aid stuff handy, dial 911, and, of course, that maternal favorite: wear clean underwear so the emergency personnel would not be shocked. I have now learned, the hard way, that the most important tip is call 911. I can also report that nobody notices underwear, clean or otherwise, when the flashing lights fill your street in the wee hours.

Just five days ago, although it seems like both this morning and weeks ago, we had a terrible medical emergency at 5 a.m. One of our daughters was in grave trouble. She is no stranger to the medical system, but this was worse.

As Ray tried to get a response from her, her sister called 911 and I threw on some clothes and headed downstairs to confine the dog and cats, as well as nab the emergency workers the instant they drove into view. My first tip: If you have a home medical emergency, live in Littleton. The dispatcher, while calmly arranging for all kinds of help, kept my other daughter, understandably extremely upset, talking until the first police officer arrived. It seemed like forever, but was probably only a couple of minutes. Time does not fly when your terrified heart is breaking.

First the two police officers, then the EMTs on the ambulance, then the paramedics from Emerson Hospital, and finally I think even the Fire Department screamed up the street, nearly blocking the early commuters. They were all quiet and competent and sensitive. While the situation was clearly very serious, they took the time to calm the family as much as possible. After the patient was carried downstairs and into the ambulance, they moved with more deliberation than speed, working on her the whole way.

Second tip: If an ambulance or other emergency vehicle comes up behind you on the highway, lights and siren blazing, for heaven's sake, get out of the way. I have previously observed selfish idiots or perhaps just plain dolts who simply don't make way. If the light is against you, yet the cross of traffic has stopped, trust me, nobody will give you a ticket for moving ahead and pulling over. I have always been careful to move over for such emergencies, even when the ambulance is coming in the opposite direction, and I think with what I know now, I would practically drive over a cliff to clear the road. Some other mother might be sitting in that passenger seat, frozen in terror, praying.

Tip number 3: Support your local community hospitals like Emerson. It is all well and good to live on the outskirts of the Medical Mecca of the Free World, but when the blood is flowing and the respiration's ragged, you will not want to place your trust in the distant Mass General or Children's, despite their renown. The Emerson Hospital emergency room, and then the critical care unit personnel, are truly miracle workers, and again, their compassion for the family was as prized as their medical skill.

Tip number 4: Develop a strong support system in advance. Cast your bread upon the waters. Help those who need it, however inconvenient it might be, because when your turn comes, others will step up to help. For us, that means the Congregational Church, but you might pick another religious group or the Garden Club or Rotary. Littleton abounds in really great people. Fine Human Beings. Just ask.

Tip number 5: Get a job in a place that is more than a paycheck. The folks at Archer's Mobil, the Lincoln Public Library and PeaceGames in Cambridge (none of whom can easily spare staff) rallied 'round despite the temporary loss of the Bracken ménage. One colleague was in the ER with us, tears streaming down her face, even before Detective Steve Ziegler left to arrange for the fire chief to bring our other daughter to us. (She recommends, incidentally, using a red pickup with lights and siren to get through rush hour traffic. Another good tip.)

Tip number 6: I don't know what agnostics and nonbelievers do, but I am a firm believer in the power of prayer. Our daughter's recovery has been nothing short of a miracle. At several points along the perilous path, when turning points were reached, we were rewarded with the best possible outcome. Rising blood pressure. Arteries and veins damaged but not destroyed irrevocably. Clear lungs. Normal brain patterns. Life.

Whether from a stray bullet, a drunk driver, a swift disease, some momentary lapse of unimaginable force, everything changes in an instant.

Tip number 7: Hug your kids now. Love them. You can't know what tomorrow will bring or when the lights and sirens will fill your street.

Life at the Bracken residence is slowly moving back to the way it was last Thursday, but a part of us will never be the same. That's okay.

Tip number 8: Sometimes you get a second chance.

Use it wisely.

'Til death do us part

Eulogy for a Friend

I couldn't go to the service, it being in the city at noon of a day when I had to care for my favorite two-year-old, but another friend told me about it and it sounded just right. If Edith had to have a funeral, of course it should start with a medley of the Broadway show tunes she loved so much. I still can't think of her in terms of dirges; it's too soon. Maybe it always will be.

"The Lord is my shepherd: I shall not want..."

She was my friend for 15 years--about the longest I've been close to anybody outside my family, longer than I've loved my husband and children. We met when I went to work for a big company in the city, sharing a tiny drab office for a while before we both got promotions (hers higher than mine, deservedly so) and shuffled around the corporate structure, she eventually staying with the firm in another department and I moving on, out past the far suburbs to have babies. When our daughter became seriously ill, Edith was one of the first we called, knowing she would be able to comfort us, and she did.

"He maketh me to lie down in green pastures..."

Edith was on the other side of childbearing from me, although I must have known her for months before I realized she was 20 years older than I--a credit to her vivacity. We held our collected breath over her daughter's college applications-- always knowing, really, she would be accepted at the best schools. Every afternoon her son called to report that he was home, and where he was heading from there. They were good kids, grown now to fine adults--she a lawyer, he with a political consulting firm in D. C., and Edith was proud of them.

"He leadeth me beside the still waters..."

I had my doubts when my desk was moved into her little room. I was a hick, a WASP from the sticks, single, footloose and fancy free, fond of country music, going to library school at night. She was a sophisticated lady, a

Jew living in a comfortable suburb, who loved classical music, concerts, foreign films. I liked the Red Sox, and she adored the Celtics--standing up at the games and cheering like a teenager. I was vaguely wary of her, one of "them" I'd been raised to mistrust because of ethnic differences, but after a while, that dissolved into a friendship that she admitted eased some of her apprehension for the future; if I could overcome my past, maybe others could too.

"He restoreth my soul..."

Our office seemed hot to me most of the time, but Edith was usually cold. Even after we convinced the maintenance department to tape plastic film over the windows in the winter, she wore heavy sweaters every day, and in the summer, too, while I was wearing as little as was seemly in such a setting. We took to eating our lunches at our desks every day, reading and talking. Everyday, I had soup and a sandwich, a salad or maybe a slice of pizza from the cafeteria, a variety, but every day, Edith unfailingly had peanut butter and bagel, coffee and cheese, maybe a pastry in the morning.

"He leadeth me in the paths of righteousness for his name's sake..."

It was because of Edith that I became a writer. She was so happy and proud when her husband had articles and a book published, and she supported his decision to leave corporate life to teach at a community college. I had always liked to write but had no plans for publication, even when a couple of professors told me that journals would probably accept class papers I'd written. When I left the company, Edith was editor of a regional library newsletter and offered me a chance to write book reviews. Thinking it was a good way to keep up with my field, I agreed. It was with great trepidation that I sent in my reviews, half expecting Edith would be inundated with letters slamming my opinions. I never got any feedback at all from them, of course, but I kept at it and at her urging,

I became a reviewer for a respected national publication--still no pay, but at least there was recognition. That was the beginning of my career.

"Yea, though I walk through the valley of the shadow of death, I will fear no evil..."

Last October, she and her husband scouted the Cape looking for intimate little inns for visits next spring. They talked about taking up golf, maybe selling the big house and moving to a more peaceful little place in the country. She thought maybe running a little public library would be a good change, and he figured he'd retire from teaching and freelance. Tuition payments were over at last and they could afford to ease up and enjoy themselves.

"For thou art with me; thy rod and thy staff, they comfort me..."

At first, when Edith got sick in November, nobody was too worried about her. She had a serious infection, but seemed to be holding her own or maybe improving a little. The worst of it was, she was in intensive care and we couldn't visit her, and tubes prevented her from talking at all, although she was awake. We tried not to bother her husband too much, but we wanted to keep up with her condition, not that it changed much. Still, we just assumed that from somewhere she would find the strength to fight off her illness. It was impossible that she would die--she was always there. I made plans to visit as soon as I was allowed, bearing a bouquet of flowers, a jar of peanut butter and a dozen bagels. I knew she'd get a kick out of that.

"Thou preparest a table before me in the presence of mine enemies."

When she slipped into a coma, we finally had to accept that her chances of recovery were slim, but nobody even at that was prepared for the call last week that she had died. She was 57.

"Thou annointest my head with oil; my cup runneth over..."

194

One fine day last spring, I was driving past the company and decided to drop in to see Edith. I don't go that way much any more, and I don't know what made me stop. She was busy but found a few minutes to chat, and we made plans to get together in a couple of months, if we could somehow mesh our schedules and find a day. But she always had tickets to something, I was always on my way somewhere else, and we never saw each other again.

"Surely goodness and mercy shall follow me all the days of my life..."

At the service, my other friend said, the rabbi eulogized Edith, someone chanted in Hebrew, and the congregation joined in reciting the Twenty-third Psalm--Jew and Gentile joined in pain and hope for a wonderful woman. I wish I had been there – maybe then I could cry. Now I just sit here and thank her silently for all she gave me and wonder if I ever gave a fraction back to her.

"And I shall dwell in the House of the Lord forever..."

Edith taught me something else, too, although I didn't know it at the time. Several years ago she grieved when a close friend of hers died much too young of cancer. She hadn't been able to visit at the end, which made it that much worse.

Now I know how she felt.

Remembering Ma: a farewell to arms

My mother-in-law died the other night. She was one of those tough German ladies, and I always said she would outlive us all. Part of me really believed it, too, but I was wrong. She would have loved hearing me admit I was wrong about something for once.

From the first it was clear that we would never have chosen each other for friends. When her 28-year-old son called her to announce, out of the clear blue, that he had met Someone and planned to be married, her first question was, "Is she Lutheran?"

I was not Lutheran. Not a good sign. I first met her a couple of days before the wedding when she and Dad got off the plane from Denver and the snob in me was disappointed. I saw an unpolished, uneducated woman who made Edith Bunker look sophisticated. So much for my being a country hick marrying a city slicker.

What I came to realize, however, is that she was a Genuine Character. Over the past 20 years we have developed a fragmented relationship, both challenged and perhaps saved by the 2,000-mile continent that separated our daily lives.

In many families one of the first crises of marriage is what to call the in-laws. My own mother, for example, had Mother Prentice (hers) and Mother Munn (his). For me, Ray's mother was always Ma.

She had been born into a German enclave near Chicago and never spoke English until she went to school; she never got past the third grade, yet she was smart in many ways. Dad lied about his age and married Ma when he was 17 and she was 21. It lasted 54 years and she bore him three sons, two of them buried as children in the Illinois soil; to salve their sadness, they adopted a fourth son: Ray. Ma was stubborn, and selfish, and controlling. When Dad announced, on their Golden Wedding anniversary, that *he* was going to be the boss for the *next* 50 years, she replied, "Yah! Boss of the toilet!"

I was raised to respect my elders, but I couldn't hold a candle to my Chinese sister-in-law when it came to the kowtow department, and Ma let me know it.

Someone who knew Ma must have coined the expression "enjoying ill health," for she had regular collections of ailments and trotted them out whenever she could for maximum attention. She had gall bladder trouble for probably 40 years, ulcers for nearly as long, and she had had TB as a young woman. It was the TB that convinced the life insurance agent that she was uninsurable. After great consideration, he agreed to sell her a policy for $250. That was many, many years ago; the life insurance agent is no doubt dead, and maybe his children as well. But Ma held on for a full 90 years.

Sometime in the late 1970s, Ma's legs gave out on her and she needed knee surgery. Apparently she was given too much anesthesia during the operation, because for a long time she was even goofier than usual. When she awoke from the surgery, she was in a room with another patient, and Ma decided that the other patient was Dad and she also decided she wanted him to do something for her. Ma couldn't understand why "he" didn't respond, so she threw her eyeglasses case at "him." Only "he" was another old lady, who instantly demanded to be moved to another room.

Ma liked bowling and fishing and was dynamite in the kitchen. Her sticky buns were famous, her potato soup out of this world (with *spaetzle,* no less — tiny dumplings), and she always made Ray chocolate chunk and cherry cookies for CARE packages. Once I asked her for the recipe for her fabulous pie crust, but when she pantomimed "three times this much shortening," holding out her cupped hand, I conceded the pie competition to her.

Ma loved kids and accepted her grandchildren unconditionally, put her heart and soul into dramatic readings of their favorite stories, and burst with pride at their every accomplishment. She also cleaned their plates when I wasn't looking so they could have dessert.

Her favorite song was "*Du, du, liegst mir im Hertzen, Du du liegst mir im Sinn. Du, du magst mir viel Schmertzen, Weisst nich vie gut Ich dir bin.*" Which loosely translated, means "You are in my heart, you are in my mind, you give me a lot of pain because you don't know how good I am for you." It was a fitting choice. I couldn't live up to her expectations and needs. Nobody could.

When Dad developed leukemia in 1979 and died three days after diagnosis, the stuffing went out of her. She had been neither happy nor pain free since that day, and her death following surgery for a broken hip, was a blessing. Her body had outlived her rational soul.

I told Lisa early this morning that Ma had died, and as we held each other and cried, I realized, to my surprise, that I'll miss her.

"Look at it this way," I said to Lisa. "Now she's where she has somebody to control again."

"Grandpa?" she asked, quavering.

"No," I replied. "God."

Amen.

If there be mermaids

There are no mermaids in the lake
Though I have sought them there —
Slicing through the cooling depths beneath the
    summer sun.
I have danced into the water, dipping fingers in the
    lapping waves,
Digging beach-seared toes into the blessed shallows.

Nor among the rows of the head-high reeds,
        Nureyev and Pavlova
Swaying golden in the autumn morning,
Their silken cattails bursting,
Giving birth in the wind, sending the seeds to scatter
    with the geese —
There are no mermaids there.

There are no mermaids in the rain,
Though some have thought them there,
In the streaks of teardrops on the windowpanes,
        seeking to come in.
Nor in the pewter pearls that etch the cobwebs and
Hang dripping from the balsam boughs —
There are no mermaids there.

There are no mermaids in the brook,
Though some have wished them there,
Flashing among the pebbles as the singing waters
        tumble past.

Nor in the quiet among the resting fishes
Waiting silent as a willow weeps —
There are no mermaids there.

Jeanne Munn Bracken

But I dream mermaids in the sea,
Slipping from stepping stone stair ledges
Into greenish infinity just before I open my eyes.

In the frothy foam of a winter Nor'easter,
Who can say there is no mermaid thrashing
Just beyond our ken?

I believe there are mermaids in the oceans,
As my daughter believes that there are unicorns
Just over the hill.

I believe there are mermaids in the oceans
As my other child believes in the magic of rainbows.
Just as she has seen rainbows granting absolution
To the storm-wrecked bay,
I have found mermaid's tears on beaches,
Shed in the depths and delivered by the waves.

I find them among the shells —
Prosaic shells with splendid names,
        Periwinkles.
        Mermaid tears.
Lyric shells with common names —
        Tiny limpets with their blue-tipped peaks.
        Iridescent slipper shells.
Fierce sea urchins clad in hair shirts,
Or honed to a stippled beauty.
        Mermaid's tears.
        Common northern whelks
                with flutes and spirals each
                more lovely then the last,
                where grains of sand can lose

201

themselves forever.

And what are we but grains of sand?
    We are the dreamers.

And here among these ocean treasurers
Are the greatest gifts of all —
        Bits of glass,
        Colored glass,
        Neptune-polished
        To a fare-thee-well,
        Placed
            Just so
                On the beach
                    For me to find
                        And dream upon.

Mermaid's tears.
        White tears burnished to skim milk opacity.
        Tears of palest green, and emeralds.
        Amber tears that hold the summer sun.
        Tears of chapel window morning glory blue.

There are mermaids in the sea.
        For these smooth brilliant gemstones
            Are their tears,
                And my dreams.

Jeanne Munn Bracken is a freelance writer and reference librarian. She is the author of *Children with Cancer: A Reference Guide for Parents* (Oxford University Press, 1986, second edition in preparation) and three editions of *It All Began With an Apple*, the history of Veryfine Products, Inc. She has also had feature articles, reviews, and commentaries published in newspapers and magazines from coast to coast. She holds a BA from the University of New Hampshire (German major, Speech and Drama minor) and an MSLS from Simmons College. She still lives in Littleton, Massachusetts, which proves how forgiving the community can be, with her husband Ray (who still makes her laugh after 35 years) and daughters Lisa and Mollie (who have never embraced the empty-nest concept) as well as three cats and an aging dog. She can be contacted on the web at

www.jeannemunnbracken.com
or
jmbracken@netway.com

Someday We'll Laugh About This Order Form

Use this convenient order form to order additional copies of
Someday We'll Laugh About This

Please Print:

Name _____

Address _____

City _____ **State** _____

Zip _____

Phone (_____ **)** _____

_____ copies of book @ $15.95 each $ _____

Postage and handling @ $3.00 per book $ _____

MA residents add 5 % tax $ _____

Total amount enclosed $ _____

Make checks payable to Molisa Press

Send to Molisa Press
P. O. Box 308 • Littleton, MA 01460-0308